D1526101

The Messy Parts

Poetry, Prose, Art and Stories

on the subject of

Motherhood

Collected by

Lola Lawrence

&

Samantha Woodbeck

ISBN: 9798373853361

Cover Art Credit and Affirmations: Lola Lawrence

All proceeds from the sale of this book are donated to:

Every Mother Counts

https://everymothercounts.org/

Photo submitted anonymously by the original photographer.

DEDICATED
WITH LOVE,
TO *EVERY* MOTHER.

The Messy Parts

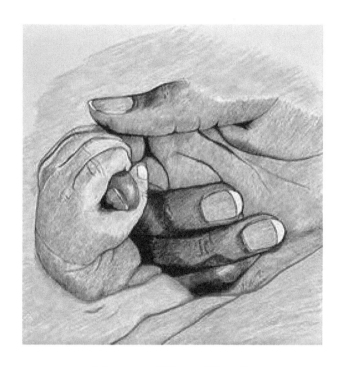

Mom and Baby Hands

Painted by Wendy Tobin

The Messy Parts

The Messy Parts

To the mothers who sacrificed so much

that a part of themselves

became the core of us.

To the mothers who worried through the night,

arose before the sun

and dressed us with affection.

To the mothers never resting.

To the mothers pinching pennies.

To the mothers juggling impossible odds nonchalantly.

To the mothers burnt from both ends and running out of wick.

This is for you.

To the mothers who dropped their own dreams

and devoted their lives

to ours.

To the mothers who fought silent wars

never spoken of.

To the mothers who stitched and sewed,

worked themselves to the bone,

kept our stomachs and souls full,

and turned ordinary spaces

into warm-hearted homes.

To the mothers too hard on themselves.

To the mothers underappreciated.

To the mothers raising gentle beasts.

To the mothers raising compassionate warriors.

To the mothers raising conquering heroes.

This is for you.

To the mother hens and momma bears

you dare not cross.

To the mothers who cheered loudest when we won,

and loved harder

when we lost.

To the mothers who wore every uniform,

carried us, cradled us, comforted us,

fueled our fiery dreams

directed and captured our most cherished memories.

Pinned Polaroid's across our hearts,

sent us out into a cold world

armed with graceful strength,

and waited anxiously for the phone to ring.

The Messy Parts

To the mothers who left the door open.

To the mothers who pray aloud for us.

To the mothers still waiting.

This is for you.

To the mothers whose lessons linger like fingerprints,

we'll make you proud.

To the mothers whose voices still echo through us,

we'll turn your words into music.

To the mothers who made us into artwork,

we're creating a beautiful life

in your honor.

This,

all of this,

is for you.

~ J. Raymond~

Christina

I had her when I was very young. It was a terrible loss. I went to the doctor multiple times and tried to tell them something was wrong. They stopped labor. Several times. By the last time I called my doctor's office hounding them that something was wrong, it was already too late.

She was gone.

I checked into the hospital, and her heartbeat was not there. They induced labor, and I had her. She was stillborn. I was diagnosed with postpartum depression.

Years later, I was given the diagnosis of post traumatic stress disorder and depression over the events.

Back then, there was no way of getting a death certificate. It was a small service, and then, nothing. I felt out of my mind with grief. I felt like anytime I wanted to talk about it, it was pushed aside or I was shunned. It caused a great deal of pain to even talk about it. It took me ten years before I was able to celebrate her birthday.

There are better nurses available now, there is more information on grief support and ways to cope with such loss. I am a daughterless mother. And it brings pain losing a baby, miscarriage, still born, or early infant loss. I have two wonderful sons, and some other kids that call me "Mom."

Even those of us that have lost a child, or those that do not have any other kids are still mothers.

~Nicole Dax~

Mothers Zephyr

The winds of change
Are oftentimes strange
A cool zephyr breeze
Moments to seize

I sat alone all night
I searched for my light
I dug into my core deep
Darkness tried to creep

But I had to stand strong
Between right and wrong
I had to hold to account
Insecurity that'd mount

I remembered my mother
Her words like no other
Your behaviour defines you
Don't do what they do...

~Purpleprincessness

The Price of Superpowers

Becoming a mom is like being transformed into someone with superpowers. Each new birth brings new superpowers. It is amazing how two arms transform into eight arms. You can now, hold a baby, talk on the phone, stir a pot of spaghetti sauce cooking on the stovetop, get your toddler some juice, throw the dog a ball, toss the laundry into the dryer, sign that school permission slip for your oldest child and set the table all in the short time of five minutes.

Well I was doing just that, being that supermom, using my superpowers, when it dawned on me the house was much too quiet. While talking with my mom on the phone attached to the wall by an eight foot long cord phone, which by the way was a rotary dial, so I guess I grew another arm, I went to check on my three kiddos. As I stretched the phone cord through the house, I found my two sons playing nicely in their bedroom. I went to my daughter's room and she was not there. Panic began to set in as I could not find my 18 month daughter. We lived in a small 900 square foot home. Where could she possibly hide? Frantically I asked my sons, "Where is your sister, I can't find her?" The boys just stared up at me and my oldest son replied, "Mom, you're holding her."

What a relief, I wasn't a bad mom, I didn't lose the baby. I only lost my mind. I guess superpowers come with a price!

~Mary Klaisner~

The Messy Parts

I was the one excited for you, though I could tell that she was worried. I offered words of encouragement, but she remained weary. I vowed to be there, and kept you in my every prayer.

Destiny came to deliver you, fortune wrapped her fist around you, fate split your world in two, and I was the one there for you.

It's hard to look in your eyes knowing you know, and though I try not to let it show, I know it too. Your deliverance is only temporary, and one day you'll be leaving me.

They say a mother's bond can't be broken, it's a love unspoken. It's a love that will withstand all, despite what may befall. Nothing can keep a mother and daughter apart. So what about my heart?

Every day, a step closer. Clinging to composure as I become the enemy, her mere presence discredits me, she reminds me personally.

I'm counting the days til you turn eighteen. I'll slip into the shadows unseen, discarded to fall apart. She'll get a brand new start. When I release my little white dove and she returns to her true mother's love.

~K.G. Carroll

Lil Pink Ballerina

By Wendy Tobin

When My World Stood Still

When my world stood still
My mother was taken ill
The lump that was found
Our fears began to hound

Cancer the report read
She consoled us instead
For us a pillar of support
She saw us all distraught

So rather than show pain
She started to fight again
She taught us to be strong
Also from right and wrong

Another lesson we learned
Another medal she earned
She fought hard and won
The cancer indeed gone

Our role model and our guide
Our mother and our pride
We can defeat every ill
If we keep a strong will

~Purpleprincessness

When my daughter was about three, we had been teaching her about sharing and giving to others. Obviously it's a challenging concept for small children. Let's be honest, even adults struggle with this as it's not in our innate, egocentric nature. We had been talking about donating toys we no longer played with to charity. We discussed how it's nice to give them to other children who aren't as fortunate and don't have any. We also reminded her that she was very blessed to always receive more toys for birthdays, Christmas, other holidays, etc. So one day I was in the kitchen preparing dinner, and I heard her say (in her adorable little three year old voice), "Mom, I want to give this one to another child. I don't need it anymore and we can get another one at a garage sale one day." I felt this sweet little spark of joy for all of the wisdom I had imparted to my obviously very kind child. As I turned around, I was immediately humbled and entertained to see her pointing to her one year old little brother. I suppose you have to start somewhere.

~Samantha Woodbeck~

At times we couldn't be more different; the calmness of water interacting with raging fire, sometimes causing water to boil, bringing all the issues to the surface, we cool off to calmer waters, all the misunderstandings evaporate, and we return to a place of love.

The things we have in common are the gift of intuition, strength, perseverance, and undying loyalty to the ones we love truly and unconditionally. You have the same desire to be free, setting your own path, making your own place in the world.

The one thing that is for certain is the true beauty of our intentions for one another is always reflected in our eyes.

You are one of the most beautiful parts of me, as you continue your journey always feel me in your heart. I am always with you every step of the way. I will support you and love you unconditionally forever. You are my baby girl, my first true love. You teach me so much, and now I pray I have equipped you to face the reality of adulthood, trusting that your journey will teach you the most beautiful lessons to become the best version of yourself, today and everyday forward.

Happy Birthday to my beautiful first born on her first day of adulthood.

~Kimberly Anne~

The Messy Parts

I've never seen a more beautiful creature

Innocent blush and new

A small part of my heart

That breathes and smiles

Delicate awe at your very existence

~Lola Lawrence~

From a Mum to Her Son

You taught me the true meaning of Love,
The very moment I became your Mum.
You made me a creator of love, of alchemy and fun.
A Mother that showers you with love as you grow and become.
You taught me how to parent, protect, nurture and guide,
Taught me what love feels like when it grows inside.
You showed me what joy really looks and feels like,
And what it feels like to love another more than life.
You made me soldier on; no matter what hands life dealt,
And I could only love you above everything else.
You enabled me to find strength that I never knew existed,
How to find peace when nothing can be predicted.
I learned how to swallow anger, pain and pride,
So, I could give you the best possible tools for life.
Together we grew hearts that knew only unconditional love,
It was you who taught me all about how to become a Mum.
How to have faith even when you are making mistakes,
How to allow another to be brave and risk take.
How to piece us back together when we crumble and break,
And how to smile even when you're afraid.
There are no words that I could arrange here on this page,
That could possibly do justice to the love and happiness you make.
You are my world and greatest teacher, my son,
And there is no greater gift than being your Mum.

~Samantha Young~

~From a Mum to Her Son - Samantha Young~

The Messy Parts

The messy parts.

The literal messy parts of motherhood.

After a few months of cleaning the messes, sans spouse in the house, I lost my mind a little.

When you mother with no safety net, eventually something gives.

In my case, it was me.

Right in the middle of another catastrophe, I just stopped cold and sank against the wall in my hallway.

I was holding a container of Clorox Wipes in my hand and I just sat there.

I had been on my way to clean my youngest son's playroom. It was covered in

mess. He was covered in mess.

It was the third time that day.

My oldest son said, "Mom, you have to get up," but the words would not compute.

"I'm going to take him into the bathroom and clean him up, okay?"

I couldn't speak.

I couldn't move.

Something inside of me broke that day.

The stress of the last three months was holding me hostage against that wall.

I was wrangling too much with no help and I knew it.

Some folks have nannies, grandparents, sitters, extended family. I was flying solo

with two very different and high needs children. One a teenager, one a toddler.

My saving grace was my teenager.

We were all we had.

In those moments, he stepped up when I could not.

The Messy Parts

I can't remember when or how I got up from that hallway and eventually
cleaned

the walls, floor, toys and windows of that playroom, but I know I did it because
it

was clean when I came out of my stupor.

Just for a while, my mind needed to break away from the stress, the
responsibility

and the chaos I had been living under.

I'd like to say my life got better after that day, but it remained the same. I
learned to

delegate better and ask for help more.

I also learned how valuable my mental health was and I made it a priority to
protect

myself so that I could be there for them and be a better me.

This motherhood is never without its stressors and you'll lose yourself to it
because

you're so good at your job of being a mom. You'll give and give and give until

there's nothing left.

But always be sure to give to yourself because you matter too.

~ Leigh Webb~

Painting by Lola Lawrence

The Messy Parts

These two souls.

Grown inside of me; a sanctuary.

Birthed outside of me; a hell.

"Mama." The greatest reward; the most devastating gift.

~B. Torres

The Devil In Motherhood

A baby, they say.

I'm joyful. Elated.

The hopes and the dreams, anticipated.

A ballerina?

A baseball star?

Doctor? Lawyer?

We'll take them so far.

In every accomplishment

There's wonder and awe

First words, first steps

First sip from a straw

"But something's not right"

The onlookers say

"You'll have to find out what is wrong, right away"

We make the appointments

The boxes are checked

"It's autism", they say

They think we'll be wrecked

They wait for the worry, the grief and the fears

The Messy Parts

They pull out the tissues, in case there are tears

In the moments that follow

The brain's running wild

What happens now, to those dreams for my child

And on, comes the light

I don't feel so bad

Those dreams for my child were not mine, to be had

There is no disappointment

No grief and no fear

Determined, I know that my mission is clear

It was never my job to fulfill hopes and dreams,

Or comply with the milestones, as the world deems

My job is to love this child without measure

This blessing, this gift is my life's greatest treasure

"Professionals" tell me

"This life will be hard

You'll need extra help, in every regard"

We'll take all the help

Whatever is needed

We'll applaud as our hope for the goals is exceeded

We'll never compare this child to another

The Messy Parts

I'll be grateful each day to be this child's mother

When I speak of this life with an autistic child

You won't see sadness

You'll note that "she smiled"

Autism is hard

But the "hard" isn't mine

The world doesn't welcome what it can not design.

My job isn't about some old dreams, long ago

Or plans that were made for a child I didn't know

The child "before autism" brought joy and elation

I won't be defeated by the devil; expectation

Old hopes and dreams

I imagine to be

A product of what was EXPECTED of me

We think we can plan for the future ahead

But a child will be happier when expectations are shed

This child has shown me

There's room for us all

The world is too big for our minds to stay small

The Messy Parts

Some folks need help, while others know ease

But all life has value, with no guarantees

The value, not measured by what one achieves

Is in love, that is given, and the love one receives

There was no promise of the child I "expected"

THIS child, THIS gift, will be well respected.

No ballerina, no baseball star.

My love, my whole heart, just as you are.

~Donna Blasi Miglino

Bearer of Stardust

Soul flowers,
seeded
deep,
within spirit.
Her waters break
and sacrifice is made;
that legs may walk,
that arms may reach,
that eyes may open,
that love…
may know itself
once more.
She is broken
and remade,
the greatest gift
is, only hers, to give.
Everything begins
and ends with her.
Keeper of the gateway.
Bearer of stardust.
Sacred womb,
garden of all
that is to be,
and of all
that is to breathe.
Mother.

~Sabian Blade~
2023

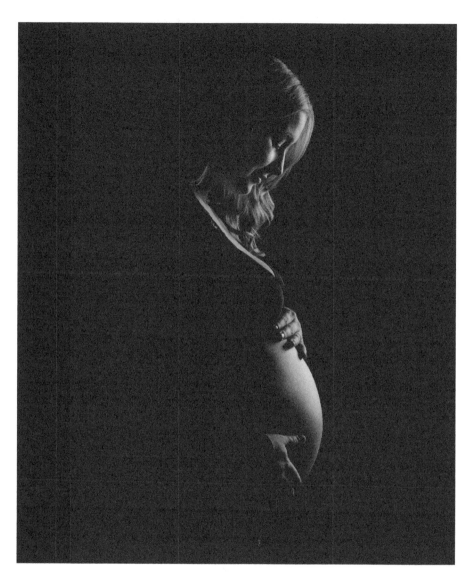

Photography: Janko Ferlic - Unsplash

Moms are magical.
Our children believe we have superpowers,
even when we feel helpless.
But look through their eyes
and it's easy to see why.
We find their smiles,
when they've had a bad day.
We make them feel better,
when they've been unwell.
We give them motivation
to never give up.
We inspire them
to reach for the stars
and to never stop dreaming.
We radiate confidence
even when we are scared inside.
Our children see our magic
when we can't see it within ourselves.
They see us move mountains
when we dry their tears,
love them unconditionally,
and help shape their beautiful souls.
They are the hope we need to believe in ourselves,
the same way they believe in us…
Powerfully.
Beyond measure.

~Samantha Woodbeck

I am a good mom.
I am everything my
kids need.

Daughter

My daughter puts on lipstick

She sits in front of the mirror
With her camera
And snaps a selfie.

It's her birthday soon
And already she is so like
Me
It's scary.

My mom would say, one day
I'll get a taste of my own medicine,
One day I'll understand
How mothers
Are born
Worrying
And we never
Stop.

And while the sins of MY mother
Are not My destiny
My sins
Are hers

But
I'll teach my daughter to write her words
In lipstick
On her thigh
Guard them like
Secrets

The Messy Parts

I'll teach her that some people are piranhas

Eating girls with poetry
Between their teeth.

I'll teach her to love fully
And when she lets go
To let it go
Fully too

That love is a lightning
But it also has wings.

I'll teach her it's ok to scream.
I'll teach her that sometimes
Its ok to regret
The things you haven't done
That some things
Should just be
Poetry

I'll teach her to make sure she's not just the poet
But the poem.

My daughter puts lipstick on
In front of the mirror
She snaps a selfie
And smiles
She's going to be 5 soon
And already she's so like Me
It's scary

~Sadie Bart

To Mother

I sat to write a piece on mothers, and have realized it is anything but simple and straightforward.

People's first thoughts on the word "mother" relate to its definition as a noun; namely, "a mother is a woman in relation to a child or children to whom she has given birth". However, in my perspective, that definition is overwhelmingly insufficient and far too simplistic and exclusionary. I prefer to examine "mother" in its context as a verb, for I find it to be a word of action: "to bring up something with care and affection or to look after kindly and protectively". I believe this to be a far more inclusive and accurate lens through which to view motherhood.

Becoming a mother is far more complex than being a woman who has given birth. Although I met this traditional definition of being a mother when I gave birth to my daughter in 2013, I was a mother long before that time. I was made to be a mother; it was a central thread woven into the very fabric of my being. I was the oldest of four children and my siblings were my training ground for the mother I would ultimately become. As I grew into a teenager and beyond into adulthood, I found myself continuing to mother and take care of my friends in various settings. To this day, I find myself mothering others (children, peers, and sometimes people older than me) in addition to my daughter. At times it is situational, but I frequently find it is characteristic of my dynamic with certain people. I don't mean to imply that this means that I try to somehow control these people or tell them what to do, it is more of a nurturing relationship that is representative of my mother's heart. It was a role I was born to play, and did so, long before I gave birth to a biological child. Motherhood may be a calling on your life without ever birthing a child.

Motherhood is a condition of the heart; and in that sense, I have known many people who are mothers that do not meet the "requirements" to be a "mother" as defined in the dictionary. But when examined through the action of mothering, you are able to find many more people who are mothers indeed. For there are many people (not gender restricted) who bring up someone/something with care and affection or who look after someone/something kindly and protectively. This may look like an adult who cares for children to whom they did not give birth. There are many single fathers who perform the role of mother daily in addition to their own. Mothering may be bringing up beloved pets with care and affection. Honestly, it might even be providing loving attentiveness to plants in a garden. For mothering is about creating and sustaining life, cultivating it in a caring and affectionate environment where it can thrive and grow.

Being a mother is a role that requires action; although giving birth to a child may technically qualify a woman to this title, the process of mothering is an involved and intentional one. A mother is someone who fulfills innumerable occupations; she may perform the services of nurse, chef, chauffeur, teacher, therapist, mediator, and friend (to name just a few) on any given day—and often before lunchtime. She does more than simply wear many hats, a mother is a breathtaking constellation of seeming contradictions. There is no fiercer warrior than a mother whose loved ones have been threatened. However, a mother's lap is one of the most comforting, soft, and safe spaces that exist in all the world. She must have the strength and structure to create a life that will protect her "children" while they are being raised. But, as any mother will tell you, it is a role that requires more flexibility than any other, for nothing can prepare a person for the infinite curveballs that a mother will be thrown in this life. Each life that is tended by a mother also is unique, and will require individualized care in order to optimally thrive.

There are dark sides to motherhood also. The concept of mother is a central one to every life, for life does not exist without a mother. However, there are many people who did not feel that they were "mothered" adequately, carrying deep wounds from the lack of "mother" in their history. There are those who did have loving mothers and have since lost them. There are mothers who have carried and lost their children. There are women who wish desperately to become mothers in the traditional sense but are unable to do so. Loss is inevitable in this life, but expanding the definition of mother beyond the traditional allows us to mitigate this pain. For if the label and role of mother isn't limited to one person, it will be much easier for needs to be met and allows people to feel more loved, supported, and cared for. I am a huge believer that it takes a village to raise a child, but I also don't think that concept should cease once adulthood is reached.

There are many people with mother's hearts in this world and we should be using them to take care of one another. If less importance were placed on the biological bond between a woman and her offspring, and greater emphasis placed on the condition of the heart and love that is offered through the act of mothering, much of the brokenness and wounding of this life could be healed. Motherhood is so much more than a job or even a state of being, it is a calling—and it is not one that is limited to adult females who have biologically birthed a child. And "mother" is not merely a title to bear, but rather a never-ending choice to actively and intentionally raise up and care for another life with affection and protection. It is something we may have been born to be, made to become, or have chosen and made manifest; nonetheless, we are all making our way together.

And so, I raise my glass in solidarity to everyone who has this heart and has chosen to answer the call...To Mother.

~Raya Soleil

Another Day's Work

As night falls and her fortress settles

(as does her mind for a brief moment in time),

her pups dreaming soundly,

you will find her singing softly with the nightingales,

letting her guard down in the quiet shades of magenta;

polishing her magic slippers

and pressing her cape for another day's work to come.

But a mother's work is never done; it rises with the moon and sets with the sun.

As does her love...immortal, feather-soft, fierce and feral.

~Ann Marie Eleazer~

18th March

I had never meant for things to end,
I thought we were forever.
Shocking how life turns things on their head:
Life away from him is better.

Sure, leaving him was terrifying,
But staying would have killed me.
Dragged down to murky depths and falling...
Not slowing: tumbling, constantly.

A searing light pierced my head and heart
Before I broke completely.
A voice inside said, "you have to start
to get back up for the baby".

That was when I knew the time had come.
I had no choice but to go.
To make a better life for my son.
To stop the madness. To say "No".

So a year ago today I left.
My life bundled in my car.
Driving away with Jude, bereft;
Our destination feeling so far.

There've been times when I questioned myself.
"How can I do this alone?"
I wasn't alone: you all helped.
I'm so grateful for the love you've shown.

~Annie Armitage

The Messy Parts

I became alive intertwined with your umbilical cord

feeding you nutrients of love

Harboring you safely inside my womb

Until you arrived, through skin divide

You were the brightest light that ever emerged from the darkness
within me .

I held you so tight even an army couldn't pry my arms from around
you.

You suckled my breasts until they were bloody and bruised , a chest
both painfully and beautifully used .

I was a broken statue of motherhood living in a body of a gender I
did not know,

A body bag filled with anger and shame

Pain was my only home until you came

I gave you life , you gave me reason

I gave you a refuge ,you gave me embrace

Unconditional love , so much joy beauty and grace

Confused on how the world would see me

Afraid of how you perceived me

would I let you down , would my arms become a ghost town filled
with only

memories of our bond .

Do I risk my happiness in fear of making you sad

do I risk our safety for the world to think I'm bad , Will it be worth
the risk to go

from mom to dad?

The Messy Parts

How can I feel alive and broken all in the same breathe , how does one create

life while another creates death

Surly this beautiful being of light would soften my hardened heart , built with

walls so high I felt like humpty dumpty falling from the Empire State

Building

And No amount of love could put me back together again

But somehow you did . With your little hands wrapped tight around

my finger ,

your hcad rcsting on my chest

It didn't matter to you what I looked liked like

To you I was the best .

You took that broken statue of motherhood and put me back together again

and again and again

You held my hand through the transition of fatherhood

as I found myself within ….

~By Willow Bodhi~

Wish I had told you "I see you." That I noticed how hard you tried. That everything you sacrificed for me was appreciated and you weren't invisible.

I wish I had told you I saw the pain you tried to hide so I could have everything I wanted.

I wish I spent more time with you instead of rolling my teenage eyes because I thought you were boring. Paid attention to the things you wanted to teach me. Had given my full attention to the little things you loved, to repay even a fraction of the times you gave my passions your all.

I wish it didn't take losing you to know how blessed I was to call you "mom."

~Lola Lawrence~

The Messy Parts

If I had a star,

I'd save it for you.

After everything

I've been through,

I'm not so sure

I'm doing this right.

There are days when I

lose total sight.

In case I fail

to heal my scar,

I'll save you mommy's

bright, healing star.

~T.B. Elden~

Never See Me Cry

They don't know I struggle,
and it's easy to see why.
They don't know I struggle
because they never see me cry.
I hold it all together,
even though sometimes,
I'm dying inside.
Crying in the shower,
or head on my steering wheel.
Drying my tears so
They're not guilty for how I feel.
It's not their fault.
I'm just tired and need a break.
They're worth so much more
than every sacrifice I make.
But it's OK for them to see
that moms cry too,
and are human beings.
Overall I'm so grateful to be present and alive.
Laughter mixed with some tears most days,
so that my beautiful children can truly thrive.

~Samantha Woodbeck

Bleeding Heart

The other mothers sit and whisper

staring like we're a TV,

eyes moving from your feeding tube

to the portable machinery.

They act like they might catch something

if they were to get too near.

The atmosphere uncomfortable

as they whisper and they sneer.

All eyes here are upon us but

not one will meet my gaze,

I try hard to ignore their looks

as my cheeks begin to blaze.

Why can't they see the precious child

beneath all her special needs,

maybe show us some compassion

instead of making my heart bleed.

~Brenda Cierniak~

Twice Blessed Is Thee

From seed, she held me near.
From seed, she herself was held…

Ancestral care given naturally,
feminine magic genetic.
Charmed
is thy family line.
Sweet and wholesome
the fruit,
tears and all…

From love, I was born.
From love, she herself was born…

The mother's womb is sacred,
healing and gentle.
Protected,
is thy heart
within her mind,
within her arms.
Earth angels need no wings.

From adversity, I flower.
From adversity, she herself, flowered…

Invisible connection,
for now and always.
Eternal,
is thy bond
within her eyes,
within her soul.
We, she and I, are one

~Sabian Blade~
    2023

Photography: Joey Thompson - Unsplash

Just One Bite

My precious child

I sometimes forget how hard it is for you

The challenges you face daily

Your struggles which are invisible to others.

But I know my child I know

That what others take for granted, simple things like eating a piece of broccoli is a massive challenge for you

You are grown now but I remember years ago when you were smaller desperately trying to get you to eat vegetables, or fruit or *anything* that wasn't either chips or pizza.

There is one particular day which I will never forget as it is scalded into my heart and soul for eternity until I leave this place.

I had bribed you with money - lots of money

Actual real cash which for an 8 year old was huge!

As I was so desperate at that time to try and get you to eat.

'Just one bite' I said

Just. one. bite, one little bite of this broccoli and you can have this money

I remember you trying so hard, how you tried to take a tiny bite but just couldn't as the texture and taste was too much for your sensitive heightened palate.

I remember you, the child who is now a grown man and an atheist dropping to your knees, right there on the kitchen floor and praying out loud with tears in your eyes asking God to help you to take a bite,

Just. one. bite of a piece of broccoli

Writing this now my own eyes are filled with tears

Because in that moment seeing you on your knees, praying with tears in your eyes I realized, I truly realized what you go through

The Messy Parts

What you go through

Every. Single. Day

And alongside the immense sadness I felt in that heart stopping moment I felt anger too.

Anger at all those well meaning people throughout your early years who didn't understand, who thought I was a too soft mother, who would say "he will eat when he is hungry" or "he is just a fussy eater, don't spoil him"

They didn't understand

They didn't see a little 8 year old child on their knees with tears in their eyes praying, literally praying to a God they didn't even fully understand yet as still so young, asking to help you to take a tiny bite

To take a bite

Just. one. bite. of a piece of broccoli

I vowed there and then, a lightbulb moment for me,

to never force, cajole, beg, or bribe you to do this again

I scooped you up off the floor, into my arms and held you

We had ice cream instead and chips and pizza and I gave you the money anyway as you tried

My god did you try!

Right there on the floor on bended knee

To take a bite, Just. one. bite

of a piece of broccoli.

~Danielle Gibbens

Always In Me

I set on a search for happiness and wondered where it would be

I looked up at the sky and thought with the big beautiful sun I could see

I was convinced until it was filled with dark cloudy gray stormy skies

I realized the sky wasn't happy as when it rained the sky also cries

I saw a beautiful young baby laughing and playing with her mother

As she had nothing to worry about, no stress, nothing that would be a bother

But as the child's mother moved aside to talk with another

The child screamed, cried and was rather quite distraught I'd discover

I kept looking around for places of happiness that I could see

But it became more and more obvious that in actual reality

Happiness isn't easily found in everything in actuality

It has to be created and that mine was entirely up to me...

~© Purpleprincessness~

The Messy Parts

We never lose words.

We just hide them away within our heart and mind.

Waiting for the right words to say at the right time.

Don't worry my child

Cause we have the moments that we shared

Even during our tough times, just know I cared

And you made me proud

Although I may never have said it out loud

Just know in my heart you are always there

~James Wesley

My feelings
are important
and valid.

A Heart Reigning Over Motherhood

Where to begin? Perhaps with the thundering heartbeat that imprinted its music deep into my core? Let's start there.

A young mother at twenty and not prepared by material means has only her heart to let reign over the winding journey through motherhood. That's where my story began, pinched between a place of youth and womanhood; that's how many other stories begin, on a path set to traverse the unknown. On this new journey of mine, "friends" were lost, doubt embedded my mind, and I felt like a sailor lost at sea with only a small compass, yet something was new and delightfully enigmatic. A sweet warmth like the tender touch that emanates gently from a morning sun stirred gently within my belly and in its ambience an ember sparked. However, the wildfire grew at the sound of that first heartbeat as I watched the jagged peaks of a tiny heart's rhythm on an ultrasound monitor. There was no denying the sudden stirring within my soul. I was consumed with a light that I swore could burn but it could be better described as unconditional love.

If only the journey through motherhood was one where every scrape, cut and bruised knee could be foreseen…would we be constantly tethered to our children, bound to the knowing of their demise? I have learned, painstakingly, that life is an ebbing and flowing creature much like the ocean, raging beautifully under one silver moon and crimson sun- it cannot be controlled wholly. We dip our toes, swim, explore and face the tides all in one day of motherhood. On October 31st, I'd had weathered almost twenty-four hours of labor to finally give birth to one beautiful, rosy-cheeked baby boy. Almost nine pounds, kicking, crying, and gasping in the fresh air of his new world, he took to the breast immediately as I hushed him into a quiet trance. You take it all in, that inevitable molding of their soul to your own. It's an invisible force but it's as real as the fresh linen wrapped around their small body and the fragrance of their soft skin. It's as real as the sounds of suckling and the tears that run down your cheeks to your exposed chest.

The Messy Parts

That day, I became a mother. What a responsibility. Your heart takes a turn once you give birth. The journey you began nine months ago that seemed to stretch forth into infinity becomes both a scenic adventure and destination: small socks, sleepy eyes, the fragility of their helpless little bodies and weight of their being against your own. Once you feel the sunrays of their soul, you become the Earth unto which they unendingly settle. Evan, my firstborn, came into the world as strong as his unfettered heartbeat; wild, stubborn, and beautiful. While the stars have seemingly aligned as my heart shines with adoration, there are routes that twist, loop and whirl into each other; there are messy parts from which motherhood can still be defined. Temper tantrums, kicking, screaming, and crying fits that permeate tensely against raw nerves, the exhaustion of staying up late to check a fevered forehead every few hours, the monotonous doctor appointments, and long "to-do" lists. Every unchecked box of what you wanted to get done during the day remaining void of its checkmark due to the strain and priority of putting that child first. The skipped shower at the end of the day you swore to yourself you'd take being replaced by bathing your little one. These messy little parts of the journey are the dips and curves.

My firstborn welcomed his little sister later in life. Her presence, a rainbow amidst any storm; sweet to the soul as one could see through her smiling eyes. Like a wind chime in a soft wind, she rang out her own tune in the world, not a clash but a serene melody though she stirs madly at times. Emberly joined her brother in the root of my existence- my soul. My heart grew even bigger to home natural instincts and motherly compassion. Once again, the valleys and mountains combined to keep the sun at astounding heights and the water beneath it. You can't have a heart full of love and not have life dare it to lose its grip during the climb. For life does, every chance it gets. It dares you to forget lilting cadences when little giggles have turned into deepening tones of pubescent boyhood. It dares you to forget the serotonin-amplifying sounds of first being called "mama." It dares you to forget your heart's sacred anthem when everything else in life becomes noisy. The preteen boy who was once merely a soft, sweet newborn shows shades of vibrant rebellion with red-cheeked temperament.

The Messy Parts

He clashes against both peace and patience by raising his voice and initiating a mama's great annoyance- backtalk. Oh, what a trip that journey becomes!

You then stand before your child, losing patience as quickly as a pot of water boils hot. It happens slowly and then quickly as your face matches his crimson defiance. You find yourself wondering "where have I gone wrong?" No longer am I the twenty-year-old pinched between youth and womanhood. I am a woman slowly and gracefully moving into older years. Yet the ferocity of passion steeps wild words, emboldening anger born from fear. It forgets at times, the wisdom and chastise finessed from the unlearning of generational traumas, all in a moment. I speak and then I yell, causing his eyes to show a whisper of fear and perhaps pain. I boil over and spill out fiery words, giving into life's taunting. I should have chosen truth over dare. He slinks back eventually and recedes but not easily, after all, he is a strong-willed child. Eventually, I sit with him in a silent room, letting my heart break and mend at the same time, doing everything I can to hear him fully. I apologize for being brash and for yelling. I let my heart guide every word and I am his sounding board. I am his mother, and I am flawed.

I hug him, I hold him; I nurture him with every imperfect piece of me, hoping my mosaic heart will somehow still shine for him perfectly. I let my mistakes breathe and I surrender my pride out into the open. I tell him "Son, I love you unconditionally." When I am wrong, I say sorry. I reminded him that even I am still learning. I begin to hear our song clearly; his strong, unfettered heart against my own drum's beating- this is where it all began and will never end. Love, in all its beauty, picks us back up and puts us together to keep us moving, traversing, and dancing hand in hand to the cacophony. I am blessed with two children who awaken the very best in me, all by the divinity of one heartbeat. Together, we will continue to find the sunniest skies. And I will keep singing "You are my sunshine, my only sunshine, you make me happy when skies are gray, you'll never know dear, how much I love you, please don't take my sunshine away." I was once a young mother at twenty, not prepared by material means for motherhood but I did let my heart reign and always will.   ~Whitney Reid~

The Messy Parts

Five,
Three,
Four little words.

"You make me feel loved."
Are five little words
That should not have made my heart cry.

"You make me feel loved."
Are five little words
That should have run
A tear-filled stream
Dry...

"you make me feel loved."
Are five little words
I am thankful for every day.

"You make me feel loved."
Are five little words
That one would think
Kept my monsters
Away...

"You make me feel loved."
Are five little words
Others may not comprehend.

"You make me feel loved."
Are five little words
A constant reminder
Of how she never could
Yet I can...

You feeling loved
Are three little words.

"I love you."
Are three more.

"You are my world."
Are four little words
Filled with enough
Faith & hope
To restore...

Inner safety to my shore.

~Anna M. Ortiz~

This poem expresses that struggle for those that may not understand what
it's like to experience this. My hope is that others feel validated and not
alone.

The Messy Parts

It's been a long, beautiful week. I let the kids stay up late last night. Tomorrow they rise early again to go back to school. While tucking Max in around midnight, & kissing him all over that face, those words hit hard. He smiled, looked at me & said, "You make me feel loved." I held it in tears. The emotions that came over me are not truly expressive in words other than "heavy." There are certain things in this life we do not, should not, need validation for. The ugly truth is this, we do. It's not the same for everyone. I suppose this was more of an epiphany than a validation of sorts. He's ten, he's never said that before, and it caught me completely off guard.

I wanted to call my dad and say, "I did it! I'm doing it. It's ok." but I can't. I certainly can't call her because she would call me dramatic, say she did the best she could, or ask me if I needed an award for being a mom. My dad, well, pretty sure he would have hugged me and just said, "Good job, pidge," and kissed me all over my face. He would have understood.

Happiness does not mean you won't have setbacks. Healthy does not mean fully healed, but better. I'll take it. I'm not where I was; that is good enough for me, even if she and I will never be...

I am a good mom to my babies.

~Anna M. Ortiz~

Wired Differently

My wires might be crossed, but I am here.

I may not speak in words, but I speak in my emotions loudly.

I may not do what is asked of me, but I do what works for me.

I am here fighting to fit into a world that was not made for me.

I am fighting to be me in a way others might see my beauty.

My heart is full even if I can't show it in a way I may think that I should.

I am who I am, wired in a way that makes me beautiful in a very different way.

See me for who I am, not the way you think I should be.

~Stephanie Houltzhouser~

Derailed

Mommy brain
Runaway train
Can't think straight
Always late
Sleep deprived
Barely alive
Needing to eat
Meltdowns on repeat
Baby's teething
I'm hardly breathing
Often confused
Less than enthused
Craving coffee
A moment for me
Haven't brushed my hair
So much for self care

~Samantha Woodbeck

A Mother's Burden

"My heart aches with every ounce of your suffering. Every pang that hits your tiny being pierces straight through me like a blade to the gut. I would do anything to take your pain from you, even add it to the overwhelming amounts I already possess. I feel so hopeless as you cry in my arms wishing for it to all go away. The burden of a mother who was forced to watch her children suffer much more pain than they ever should have had to."

~Jenna Lynn

Reoccurring Heartbreak

A sudden traumatic experience occurred, past
tense
Scars that were etched into my soul have still not
healed fully deep down
as anxiety continues to reside in the pit of my
hollow stomach, not loosening the reins
I'm often overwhelmed, full of deep emotions
that slice through my heart
time and time again
hitting me at the most unexpected moments
Swirling thoughts run rampant in my mind
of losing someone you love forever
It has a lasting impact on who you are
Uncomfortableness, discomfort
churns within my body, never fully recovering,
always waiting for the next time
The next onslaught of emotions,
of memories, and painful realities
as sadness and never ending darkness
is but one step away
waiting to take over at any moment
Pulling me back through the gates of hell
in the blink of an eye
Always watching for triggers
Always questioning
Always waiting
for the next time

~Tegan Matthews, TGN Poetry~

Photo by Tegan Matthews, TGN Poetry

Jewels of the Sea

If I had our lives to live over,
I would raise you by the sea,
where you could chase the cobalt waves
and in the salty air, be free.

And we would hunt for ocean treasure
along driftwood lined shores,
our pockets filled with shells and stones,
seeking selkie pelts of lore.

We'd walk past candy-coloured houses
alongside old cobbled roads,
and listen to the ernes cry out,
as they circle fishing boats.

We would live in a cape cottage,
with wisdom in its weathered walls,
filling it with lilting folk songs,
laughter ringing through the halls.

All your battles would be fantasy,
against only mythic foes,
defeating mock leviathans
and banishing the shadows.

And I would give you gifts of wishes
in place of fragmented dreams,
and prove that even broken things
become jewels by the sea.
~ Jennifer Torvalson
(Dedicated to Liam, Logan and Faethe)

Before You

I became someone else when you came along,
Shedding so much of all that I knew,
Friends I saw often, I rarely saw anymore,
I no longer wanted to do what they chose to do.

Instead of late nights and karaoke,
I stayed home singing lullabies and old rhymes,
With the most handsome boy held safe in my arms,
Wishing that I could somehow freeze time.

I learned to be selfless, courageous, and brave,
Realized I was now cautious of whom I could trust,
Because for a short time, I'm the keeper of treasure,
Of an innocent soul and a heart true and just.

Books, toys, and games – I've bought plenty,
But things were never truly what made you smile,
It was me you wanted, my time, and my love,
Even now when you ask if I can play for a while.

There isn't much time left before you are grown,
I know you'll be a good man, just wait and see.
I'll never have words to tell you how much
Being your "Mom" is a privilege to me.

I cannot, and will not, ever go back,
To being the person I was before you.
It's funny how someone, once so tiny and small,
Became the greatest love my heart ever knew.

~Charlene Ann Benoit

A Mother's Love

The power of a mother's heart
Holds an unconditional desire,

Her love is simply a treasure of resilience,
Where you shall be treated
At the highest magnitude.

Trajectories that life sets us,
Are overcome with a mother's support.

Being a gentleman today,
Is the chivalry that she instilled us with.

In the end,
There is no greater loss
In having your heart broken...
From a mother.

~Alshaad Kara.

Buckle Up, It's a Journey!

Motherhood is the scariest but most joyful travel of life. Each day is a new journey. Having mom friends does help. It's kind of like having a tour guide but your journey and theirs are very different and no two can ever be replicated. Take each second, minute, and hour...each day, month, and year as they happen. Cherish the happy and embrace the sad because those days will happen too. Time goes fast. And nothing stays forever. Your children will consume your every being from the moment of conception and every day forth. It's love in its purest, raw, and ever so real form.

Mom of two,
~Jessica Wateski

Synchronized Love

~I still yearn for those yesterdays
Days of Picture Perfect Clarity
Frozen moments in time

~Leaving an indelible mark on my Soul
And a tattoo of Love on my Heart

~A still-shot of three Black teenage boys
On the brink of manhood
Manhood that would ultimately approach as fast as the blink of an eye

~Three black teenage boys
Walking down the mean streets of
New Orleans
With lessons ahead that included both Algebra as well as advanced
studies for survival in the hood

~But for this brief moment
of this morning
Just like all of the other school day mornings -
Those Three Black Teenage boys
Turned around in unison
As if they were conjoined triplets
Prompted by a rhythm from a place only understood between a Mother
and her sons

~Those three Black Teenage Boys from the Hood
But not of the Hood -
Turned in unison
And waved Goodbye with Gold Medal synchronized waves

~I eagerly awaited those waves like a child awaiting Christmas Morn
Days of Picture Perfect Clarity
Frozen moments in time
I still yearn for those yesterdays

~Roslyn Black

The Messy Parts

And so I'll sit and care for you; quietly from afar.
And though I bleed in secrecy and know that it will scar.
It makes me smile to know at least, you're not completely gone.
I'm fine burning this candle dear, in silence if it's wrong.

You'll never know for sure my love, if closed the door remains.
But secretly I pray one day, you learn what it retains.
This heart that loves you free of expectation - free of guilt.
'Cause matters not the outcome, but all that that we have built.

Harmonic favor may be what awaits us in the end.
But really nothing matters, as long as you're my friend.

Written from a place of love and caring for a mother.

~Anton P. Vasilyev

The Messy Parts

A Mother's Love

My hopes for your futures are…
That you turn into lovely adults
That you smile often
And love lives within all your hearts
That the world doesn't make you jagged and mean
That you are open and kindhearted
You are fearless and free
I know you watch everything I do
Some days I find it difficult to be the role model you all need
I know I'm meant to be better and stronger
I keep trying though
Aiming for the stars
Knowing I am
Your everything
That you all need me to be
And I keep trying
Like a hamster on a wheel
Working my hardest and trying my best
To be the mother you need and want
I am trying to be a great mother
But some days I fear I fail
I continue on
Knowing I will not quit
I will always be here for you all
And I will love you with every shred of my being
Until my last breath
That is my promise to you all
That I will keep trying
I will be your rock
I am stoic
It is my life's work to be here for you all
To be the mother you all deserve
Even though some days are messy
Even when I lose my temper and I shout
Even on days when my cooking isn't quite as good as Daddy's

The Messy Parts

I'm still here
Being your Mummy
Working my hardest to show you all my love
You never ending love
This unwavering mothers love
That I show you all daily
Through my hugs and my laughter
Through my hidden tears
Even when I don't feel like I am up to the job of being your mummy
That maybe I'm not quite good enough to be your mother
These horrid thoughts that plague me daily
I am still here though
Turning up
Being present
I hope you all see
That I am trying my very best
To be the best mummy I can be
I hope you all see that
And you see the real me
The loving mummy
But my point is
I am trying my best to be everything to everyone
And I will continue to do this
Whilst I hold on with the tightest of grips
I won't leave you
I love you all
You are my reason for being
My life
My lifeline
The reason my heart beats
My unflinching love
A mothers love

~MK AC Nevin-Crooks
@LoveLifePoet13
(Mommy of four beautiful humans and one fur baby)

Planting a Smile

If you've ever been into the library
You may find something left by me
A bookworm born and meant to be
I left hope in books for people to see

I spent my childhood and early years
Seeing words bringing pain and tears
As I often hid out in the library to read
I started planting a smile for those in need

I'm sure much to many librarians dismay
I tried my best to make sadness go away
I would pick roses from my front garden
Hoping my mother would grant me pardon

I would leave their petals in many books
For the sad book readers hiding in nooks
Who read silently as a means of escape
Fighting inner battles without a cape

Not just petals but little love/kind notes
To show them beauty and that hope floats
I was not a superhero just plain old me
Who wanted to see someone smile beautifully...

~Purpleprincessness

NB: First and foremost my sincerest apologies to my mother who didn't until recently know who her rose thief was. Also to librarians who found them and my penciled notes of love, kindness and support and saw them as vandalizing. In my innocence it was my way of silently planting a smile...

The Owl

It is not the wide meadows
Where you reside
I've run through every one, searching

I've gone to the sea,
to bring you to me
That left me bereft and hurting

In times when I'm brave
I visit your grave ...

But deep in the forest of dark
It is not the call of the lark
Nor is it birdsong so sweet
Or the crow's "caw" on repeat

I know I'll never see you
Nature's camouflage protects
I'd settle just to hear one "hoo"
The Owl's twice projects

So I cease all movement and listen
Close my eyes and find my center
Fine tune my ears to nature
So quiet is the sound of winter

Then there in moon shadow I stand
Barely breathing, my heart in my hand
Finally the blessing, my finest
blessing, you
Far, far away - a distant Owl's "hoo"

~Antoinette Salge
© Shē 2022

I make time
to celebrate
myself.

Mothering is a Mission Field

Over this past year, I have been studying the book of 1 Peter as I have
been leading a small group of ladies in a Bible study each Wednesday,
and then a neighborhood group each Monday night! One of the
groups is comprised of ladies similar to my age and older, so I also
joined the other small group because there are a couple of ladies
younger than me and they live within my neighborhood!! There are
many verses in Scripture that talk about the need for followers of Christ
to get together and support each other just as our human body has
many parts that need to work together to function properly. During the
past two days, I read a verse that also explains why we need to share our
experiences and encouragement with one another. 1 Peter 5:11 says,
"Resist the devil, firm in your faith, knowing that the same kinds of
suffering are being experienced by your brotherhood throughout the
world." God planned for us to live in community with other followers
of Christ in order to resist Satan and to be able to stand firm in our
faith because suffering and trials are inevitable!

-Romans 12:1-2 – "Therefore, I urge you, brothers and sisters, in view
of God's mercy, to offer your bodies as a living sacrifice, holy and
pleasing to God—this is your true and proper worship. Do not
conform to the pattern of this world, but be transformed by the
renewing of your mind, that you may prove what is that good and
acceptable and perfect will of God."

As mothers, we definitely learn to be "a living sacrifice" starting with
pregnancy and labor. We get a crash course on becoming selfless,
which is easy once we hold that precious newborn and then fall in love
with this new baby. Once we become sleep deprived and every waking
moment is consumed with caring for children, the constant sacrifice
starts up again. How do we deal with the constant sacrifice required to
be a mother? As a woman who had her first child 33 years ago, I want
to encourage you to remember that life goes by fast, so don't waste the

wonderful stages in your children's lives wishing you could move out of the one you are in and get onto the next one. To me, it already feels like it was a lifetime ago when my kids were little, and I miss those special moments. I'm not saying that positive thinking on this bit of advice will make things easy. As it says in the verse above, we need "the God of mercy" to give us guidance through the Bible and His Holy Spirit within us, which is "the renewing of our minds", in order to be transformed and God will help us be that living sacrifice. I stay involved in Bible Studies in order to make reading the Bible and encouraging others a priority in my life.

You also need to gather some support so you can have a break from the kids to relax, spend time with your husband, and exercise regularly. I had always wanted to learn to paint landscapes, so every Thursday night I would have dinner on the table when my husband came home from work and I would leave for "Paint Night" at my dad's home. My kids loved their special night as they would often sing and dance to "Daddy's songs," our old 70's music.

Another way I gathered support was to regularly have date nights with my husband and to plan Anniversary trips. Your marriage is the foundation of your family, so it needs to be a priority or your foundation will crack! It is also important to have at least one older woman who has been through the child rearing stage you are going through to encourage you and give you advice. Getting together with ladies your own age is equally important.

The second verse talks about "not being conformed to this world but being transformed by the renewing of your minds". The opposite is also true. You will be conformed to the patterns of this world if you aren't making it a priority to be transformed by renewing your mind. You can't be transformed if you aren't daily renewing your mind by reading the Bible, listening to it, singing it, meditating on it! You can't shepherd your child's heart if you aren't constantly being taught by the Great Shepherd! It is so important to take the time and energy to teach your kids to examine their hearts to see if they are walking by the flesh or the Spirit. Use hard situations and conflicts that reveal who they are worshiping, to discuss how they are worshiping themselves and their kingdoms rather than seeking first the kingdom of God and His righteousness. If you don't take these opportunities to discuss how sins they are falling into reveal a heart that is worshiping self rather than God, they will have a false sense of security that they just need to do certain things externally to be a follower of Christ.

When my children were young, I was feeling very overwhelmed and pulled in too many directions. I decided to stay home full-time and didn't continue pursuing my career until the kids were in high school and then I worked part-time. Mothering was my mission field during those years, and I felt like this was a very valuable job. I loved being able to have those years to focus my time and energy on my family and being a homemaker. After my children finished high school, I had plenty of years to continue growing in my career and working full-time.

~Christina Miner~

The Messy Parts

Momma…

just know you are enough.

When it all falls apart

When you feel inadequate

When you miss who you thought you'd be

You…are…enough.

~Lola Lawrence~

Sisters
Painted by Wendy Tobin

A Mother's Unconditional Love

She asked her mother crying, 'but mum, I prayed So much for this, what went wrong?' Her mother addressed her adult heartbroken daughter lovingly. A mother's prayer, my beautiful angel. A mother always prays for the betterment of her children. She prays for you to get nothing less than the best. She paused for a moment and said 'So mum, my prayers were not answered? Her mother softly replied "Some prayers are better off not being answered, as ultimately they were bad for us. A calmness came over her, and her mother sensing this said 'You deserve better and better is looking for you, patience beautiful angel.... patience.

~Purpleprincessness

I am strong,
but know its ok to
be vulnerable.

In a Heartbeat

No one told me
The sound of a heartbeat
would change my life forever.
No one told me there's no real way
to prepare to be a mother.

No one told me
it would be this hard.
The constant fear.
The vast unknown.
The always unexpected.
The non stop worry.
The never ending exhaustion.

No one warned me
that it would take such a toll.
The sleepless nights.
The endless tomorrows.
The personal sacrifice.
The physical pain and mental strain
The emotional roller coaster
of just trying to stay sane.

No one told me
that one day I'd love so hard
that all of that would seem irrelevant,
when looking in the eyes of my children,
these miracles that are Heaven sent.

The Messy Parts

No one told me about the hard stuff.
The constant struggles of the heart,
and battles inside my soul.
That all this chaos
somehow works together,
to continue making me whole.

No one told me.

But even if they did,
it wouldn't have made a difference.
It makes no logical sense.
Being a mom,
even in broken pieces
makes me feel complete.
I'm learning to love the messiest of parts.
And I'd do it all over again
in one single beat of my mama heart.

~Samantha Woodbeck

The Messy Parts

Someone came into my life but only for a season, always at a distance.

I am a mom for life.

I have taken every opportunity and sacrifice to be present daily.

I examine my feelings.

Regrets? Perhaps.

I should have had more courage.

Mistakes? No, rather careless decisions.

Will I ever not feel bad about them or feel that sense of loss?

So what would that one thing be if I could turn back time?

Would I have deep discussions and listen to feelings rather than just rip

them from family, schools and friends?

I would find the strength and courage to fix my broken pieces.

We recall and share experiences so they will undoubtedly make better

choices.

I have a great life despite my "less-than-perfect" choices and I have

much to be grateful for.

I have salvation, self-compassion and I am improved.

Those that have already left the footprints will guide you in which ones

not to follow.

Is it possible to really leave your past behind?

~A grandmother~

The Messy Parts

I wish I was better

not this flawed creature

I wish I wasn't so tired

I wish I could bend time

so I had more with you

I wish I gave you more

but some days momma feels empty

there are days I cry all day

until you come home

and then slip on the mask

so you don't see my struggle

I wish I were strong enough

to let you see me be human

but mommas aren't supposed to be human

we are never supposed to break

Never supposed to falter

we hold whole world's cupped in sweaty palms

while still trying to not fall down

~Lola Lawrence~

Tribute to Tyler

This poem is a tribute to my nephew Tyler Patrick. Birth April 16, 1998, Our Angel May 17, 1998. Tyler was born with Trisomy 18 also known as Edwards Syndrome. It is a very severe chromosomal condition resulting from having three copies of chromosome 18. Tyler was a precious gift to our family.

There are no words to express how our lives changed due to his existence and the void of his existence. Our sweet boy will always remain in our hearts. The expressed words below are my experience. My sister, my brother-in-law, and their children live the story.

Heartending

Not my story, just my experience
Though I mourn for the void of our Tyler's existence

The grief of my sister as her life broke apart
Tore at the very core of my heart

So selfless and strong she carried her pregnancy
In hopes that the medical team were mistaken genetically

These words can't portray or even convey
How darkness engulfed our world that day

Siblings strong bonded as if hearts are shared
The loss of our Tyler left us shattered and impaired

Numb and angry, not comprehending
How cruel of a world to cause pain so heartending

Not my story, just my experience
So painful a loss of our Tyler's existence

~Mary Klaisner (Just. Be.)

Keep me safe

Monsters hide in many places
neighbors, friends, family and kind faces
Don't let your guard down please keep me from danger
Not all evil lurks just in a stranger
Secrets, threats, lies from people you trust
Wanting to satisfy their sickly gross lust
You may not have known, yet the signs were there
I was too afraid to speak of the pain that I bare
My small child mind could not comprehend
Not understanding, I was unable to fend
Years of unworthiness and low self esteem
Robbed me of wanting or achieving a dream
Survival was my mission to make it through life
Alone and afraid my soul felt as if cut with a knife
Many years of pretending and living the lie
Led me down roads I chose because I much rather die
Will I ever forget will I ever be whole
I'm striving to finally arrive at that goal
So parents and caregivers don't let down your guard
Keep the monsters away and out of your yard
Let your children be safe to be kids and grow strong
So the words that I'm writing won't be their song

Keep them safe

~Anonymous~

Aubrey

Oh how I feared this monster growing inside of me. I just knew it would be the death of me. A girl they said, filling me with dread. I could already see she'll look just like me. She'll be just as mean. A terrible temper, get everything with big eyes and a whimper. Certainly, birthing my enemy. So it was odd to see she looked nothing like me. No dark eyes, or hair.

In fact she had no hair, anywhere.

And when it grew, eventually...

she grew into a blue eyed blondie.

Oh, how I love this monster of mine

walking beside me.

I just know she'll be

better than I can ever be. I can already see she'll love compassionately, with a heart full of empathy. She's the sweetest thing, she's my girl, my Aubrey, and she deserves everything.

~K.G. Carroll~

The Messy Parts

Our Third Summer

Impressive you are

my favorite tiny soul

Loving every moment

on a sunny beach stroll

Words never stop

leaving your lips

Silly pictures are taken

shaking your hips

Your eyes

Your nose

Glowing hair

Crossed toes

Are a sight to be seen

in the sparkling sun

You're a barrel of laughs

and bowls filled with fun

I adore our adventures

seeing the world through your eyes

I'm sure in the future

we will be choked full of sighs

The Messy Parts

You will rule the world

one brilliant day, it's true

But for now be creative

without feeling blue

Please stay little

for as long as you'd like

We'd all prefer you

to be forever a tyke

~Tegan Matthews~

"I truly believe that my children teach me more about life and love than I will ever be able to teach them. Children view the world in such a unique and beautiful way. As we grow into adulthood that part of us gets slowly stripped away as the rose colored glasses slip from our face, but if you're lucky enough to be a mother you get to experience it again by seeing life through the eyes of your child."

~Jenna Lynn~

The Messy Parts

Madison

She's fierce. She's strong.

A true warrior in the making.

Her unique mind never stops thinking.

I've watched her everyday,

from her first kicks to one day her first kiss.

Her will is strong, her temper often short...

She's a true force to be reckoned with and she needn't ever doubt

that she was made in his image,

so purposefully created.

Shared with me to teach me the real way to live.

To be kind, bold, and courageous,

for such a time as this.

Love, Mom

~Samantha Woodbeck~

(Watercolor painting background by Madison on affirmation pages)

Pink-gummed Grin

You never really mentally prepare yourself
To be puked on, peed on, pooped on
By a little toothless human
Who can't speak a word beyond goo-goos and ga-gas,
Who can't stand, let alone walk.

But that smile...
That wide, pink-gummed grin
That holds all of the love and trust in this world –
It's that smile that makes it all worth it.

~Charlene Ann Benoit~

The Messy Parts

Such is her beauty

Love's seeds are planted within

Her womb is sacred

~Sabian Blade~

2023

Photographer: Mustafa Omar - Unsplash

The Messy Parts

Sometimes when I pray to God, he has to tell me no.
Why he has to tell me this, someday I'll get to know.

Why do families have to mourn a life that was too shortly lived?
When they had so much more to see and so much more to give.

Hey answered me, "My child, it's love for them I show.
I took them from their suffering, the pain you couldn't know."

"They are safe with me in heaven now. It's such a peaceful place. If you
could only see them now with a smile upon their face."

Tears are for the living. A way to wash the soul. To cleanse the burden
that you carry, sometimes until you're old.

I asked him how he could take a child so innocent, sweet and small.
He replied, "I didn't take her. She responded to my call."

In memory of Bergan Jean Koehler.
~Written by Stacey Miller-Sommerfeld

I'm ashamed to admit I don't "got this"

And yet I have to do it

Because there is no one else

~Lola Lawrence~

The Messy Parts

Oh Sweet Mama...

I see you. It's another day and the coffee might not be strong enough this time. If only we could power ourselves on a combination of childrens' laughter, occasional meltdowns, spilled food, and the energy they seem to have endless supplies of. The laundry is piling up, the floors are sticky again. The dishes fill the sink and there are toys everywhere. The phone is ringing, but you dare not answer it because it's sure to trigger some extra craziness. You haven't showered yet, your hair is in a messy bun, but not the cute kind you see on social media. The kind that looks like you just walked away from a train wreck (otherwise known as your living room) after your kids dumped out every toy bin in the house. Did you even remember to eat today? No, your toddler's goldfish don't count. At least add a graham cracker or two for goodness sake. There are a million things to do, but all your kids want is for you to sit down and play. To read, laugh, sing, and just be present with them in these moments. You ignore all the rest (the best you can, because it doesn't magically go away) and focus on them. Undoubtedly, they are the most important work of your life. All this and it's not even naptime yet. Then there's dinner, and more dishes, and more laundry, more messes, giggles, stories, and tantrums all mixed in. Every single day for what feels like forever. Oh how us mamas have been there, and many of us still are. They say we'll miss these moments. They say to let the other things go. The house can wait. They say time goes by too quickly. And guess what? They are right. However, it's hard to see into the future, when you can't see past the next hour because you're sleep deprived and exhausted. The baby is teething, the toddler is potty training, and your school-age child is having trouble learning how to read and make friends. Your brain is constantly on overload. You absolutely can let things go, but for how long? The laundry fairy never seems to visit, so there is only so much you can let pile up.

The Messy Parts

The house can definitely wait, but it's hard to meet everyone's needs when things are chaotic for too long. Everyone needs something and only you know where it's at at any given moment. Oh, and last I checked, dinner doesn't make itself. Time does go by too quickly. There is nothing we can do to change that unforgiving fact. It's such a crazy balance to enjoy and capture all of the moments and milestones, while living each day in what feels like endless survival mode. We drain our energy and prioritize our families while neglecting our own needs, often without even knowing it until it's too late and we are chronically exhausted.

I see you, mama. I see myself and the whole sisterhood of moms that have survived everything that motherhood has thrown at us, if only by the skin of our teeth. We are doing the most important work, even when we can't see it through the havoc and mayhem. We see the mess, but our kids only see us. May we speak life into their very souls and show them unconditional love…

Even on the messiest days.

~Samantha Woodbeck

The Messy Parts

Your Love Through My Eyes

You Called Me *"Your Biggest Miracle"*,
The Value of Those Words Are Far Greater Than Any
"I Love You" That I've Ever Received From
AnyOne.
You Called Me *"Your Most Visible Answered Prayer"*,
If Those Words Were The Only Spoken Words You'd of Ever Said To Me,
I Would Still Know Exactly What It Is I Mean To You, How Your Love For Me Was
Far From Cumbersome.
Being Extremely Tangled From Within Brought Intense Drastic Measures As To
Decide Between You & I Who Would
Be The One.
Now I Know What It Means To Live For Someone Else Or To Give Up Yourself.
Everything Good About Me Is Because of You. You're Faith in Me Alone Has Taught
Me To Overcome.
And When In Times of Dismay,
I Try to Fathom The Courage It Took To Make The First Place I Opened My Eyes
To Was Our Home.
No Words or Actions Will Ever Describe What All You've
Taught Me or What It Is You Mean To Me.
Nothing In This World Comes Close,
Only The Love That Comes From Above is Parallel to Ours.
Almost Identical to *God's Love* For HIS Son.
I'll Never Grow Tiresome on Doing The Big & Little Chores, Even Now As An
Adult & Living in Different Households.
You've Never Given Up On Me, Even When I Made Bad Decisions & Didnt Make
You Proud.
Your Love Remained The Same.
I'm Thankful Everyday That I Am Granted
With You Under The Sun.
The Time Borrowed With You Here On Earth Is Precious & I Hold It Dearly To My
Heart,
But Nor Life or Death Shall Keep Us Apart
For Love Conquers All Therefore,
Our Journey Together Will Never Be Done.

To: My Beautiful Rose,
Rosalinda Morales .
From: Joshua Morales.

Breastfeeding

My breast is the food for my baby.
It encapsulates the whole process
Of motherhood.

The relationship shared is
Beyond the conifers...

My breasts can be victims
Of breaststroke,
Surviving cancer at any tip of time.

The relationship shared
Between them and me
Is beyond the conifers...

They feed, feel and flow down
Every food,
For my baby.

~Alshaad Kara

My Fall

Don't cry Mama, I know you fear losing your entire world but that might not happen. Make yourself laugh Mama, and no matter which way the tide ebbs and flows, be a part of everything, and be grateful for the tears. Trust that you can get through everything. Stay positive Mama, no matter what. The love you give away is the love you keep.

~Nicole Dax~

The Messy Parts

My baby lay upon my chest. He finds it his place to rest.

So calm, sweet and loving, my heart is overwhelming. So innocent, not knowing what the world has coming for him. I watched him grow, I wiped his tears and helped him overcome his fears. He played sports and had lots of friends, but his good times were coming to an end. He met a girl and had two kids. Life was good, my heart was full. My grand babies had started school.

Then one day his wife just left, tore his heart out of his chest. My heart raced seeing the look on his face. Time flashed back to his safe place. One time, long ago he layed on my chest with a safe place to rest. My powers were gone as far as fixing things. I prayed to God he'd find his wings.

It didn't end there, the world seemed bare. Things got dark, unable to repair. All of these years I was there, but now with the drugs I don't compare. I feel lost, in a dark place, now all I want is my space.

For motherhood took my best. I miss that baby upon my chest. Ten years later I have some hope, he's clean and sober with no more dope. Now he calls me everyday telling me what I'd always dreamed he'd say.

"I love you mom and thank you so much. You saved my life and you're my clutch."

From happy to sad and good to bad, don't ever give up on a child you had.

~Lisa Williams Freitas~

Painting by Wendy Tobin

Take Me Back

Take me back to the moments
when holding them close was all it took.
When kisses on scraped knees made everything better.
When a nap fixed everything
and life would start all over again upon
awakening.

Take me back to that make-believe time
of pirates, cowboys, and princesses.
Take me back when it was their toys that were broken,
and not their hearts.
When their play was innocent and full of dreams.
When turning on the light made nightmares go away.

Take me back to when my arms were enough
to shelter them from this harsh world.

Now as they grow, I hope they know,
no matter how far away they go from home,
The same arms will be here
full of love,
and always waiting to take them back.

~Samantha Woodbeck~

April 15, 2017 - 8:10am

The exact moment my mother left this earth. It was the day before Easter, mom's favorite holiday; the last holiday we had spent together seven years before. I was beside her holding her frail hand, after suffering alongside her, from the silence between us in the hospital for ten days as she was unable to speak. I drove myself home over two hours away, after she passed, and almost crashed once or twice as I was blinded by my tears and the sunlight. But that night I looked up at the sunset and all of its golden glory and I smiled, knowing she was up there, and that she was finally at peace. And that she too, from up in the heavens was looking down, smiling right back at me.

~Athena Twila~

The Messy Parts

Tired of Being Tired?

I'm here to write this because I am a mother and I got tired. No, not tired of my children, but tired of mothering in general and those that I shouldn't have had to.

In life a woman creates life with a man, and a lot of times that becomes her partner as well as the father of her children. Great blessing right, when two people create lives and stick together? But what if they don't stay?

In my instance I had felt I mothered my partner, my spouse, my children's father, and I got so tired. I did not feel we were equals nor did I feel like the lover I should be.

So you guessed it, things happened, distance pushed further and further, until I sat there looking at the man I once loved with sad and lonely eyes, no feelings left in my heart. Don't get me wrong he's a good dad but I was tired of mothering him in ways only my children should have needed.

Here's where motherhood got really hard and painful. The day came, I was checked out of my marriage and usually when that happens one parent leaves the resident. That parent was me. I'll never forget the day, til my last breath, sitting with both our children trying to explain what was happening. They were ages 10 and 6. Young but not young to the point of not understanding family dynamics were changing. My spouse, at the time, and I sat with the two of them trying to keep our emotions in check. I looked both of them in their big beautiful, though tearfilled eyes and said, "I love you both very much but mommy is moving out of the house." No other words exchanged at that moment. We both sat and explained things had changed.

I never wanted to be selfish and till this day it still kills me that I come home to an empty house without hearing mom 9 bazillion times a day. However, we gave them a choice because it wasn't their fault and we did not want to disrupt their life because of our indifferences. It was explained that if they moved with mommy they would be leaving their childhood home, the street they were growing up on, change of schools, and a possible loss of friends. Again, though they were reassured they could come see me anytime, I would come get them, every weekend with me, and every other week during the summer.

Even with all the positive reinforcements and normalcy we tried to give, I as a mother felt I abandoned them. It hurt and still hurts so bad.

Both my son and daughter chose to stay with their father, if you didn't figure that part out yet. I was not mad whatsoever, deeply hurt, but I understood that this kind of life change could alter their entire future and it was possible that it wouldn't be for the better. So I put my feelings on the back burner, and reassured them, I am one call away and (a 7 minute drive).

My ex husband and I still today try to provide them with stability and we attend their events together. It does get rocky from time to time as we have our differences of feelings but that's another story for another time.

So my message to any parent that may go through a divorce or separation; remember it is not about your feelings or self. It is putting your children and their wants and needs above your own. It is showing them how strong a family can be even if not all under one roof. But the most important thing is showing them how much you love them.

I think I'm showing my children each and everyday how much I love them, with everything I do and not letting them see or know how badly I'm broken inside without them here with me each and everyday. But with that said, I also know how grateful I am to be a mom/parent and know that I can jump in my car and be with them. Some parents; mom's and dad's, do not get that opportunity at all.

Remember it can always be so much worse.

From one tired mom to the next hang in there, better days to come. And they will.

~Jessica Wateski~

Mother Nature

Sunrise eyes bring life to the cosmos

Sleeping seeds bloom into smiles

I get to bare witness to infinite creation

Recycled radiance

An eco-friendly elegance

All before breakfast

Watching kids melt to shadows

Following closely to devotion

A connection that heals boo-boos with a kiss

Bring storybooks to life

Fueling imagination

Snuggling sweet dreams into existence

Just to repeat the next day

A mother's nature is transcendent

~TK~

@impressions_in_ink

Mama.

You gave me life

while sacrificing your own.

Nurtured me as a baby,

and long after I was grown.

You were my biggest fan,

and taught me what it means to love.

You've made me laugh until I cried;

you're truly what happy tears are made of.

You watched me dream,

and reach for the stars,

You're always with me,

no matter how far.

You held my hand,

but never let go of my heart.

Even in death,

we'll never be apart.

In every life storm,

you remained the calm.

I love you now and always,

my guardian angel,

and forever…

My mom.

~Samantha Woodbeck~

The Messy Parts

Those That Lurk

The greatest healing I ever did

was allowing my trauma to join forces

with my heart and soul

in order to arm my children with weapons

against masked monsters, sly

foxes and wolves in sheep's clothing.

Those lurking in disguise often appear

to have trusting eyes and loving

smiles,

but some have hidden horns

and kisses tasting of prickly thorns,

roses nourished with lies,

nightmares awash in nursery rhythms

and haunting things swept under the rug.

~Ann Marie Eleazer~

The Leader of the Moon

"Isn't the moon beautiful?"

I asked softly, not really expecting her to answer, to understand. How could I expect such comprehension from just a tiny girl?

"That's my moon." She says proudly.

I didn't say anything, but glanced at her quizzically, before letting my eyes slide back to the glowing orb before us.

"I'm the leader of the moon." She announces, still staring at me.

Surprised, I found myself asking, "Oh? How's that?"

She rolls her eyes at me and says, "Because, mamma. He follows me everywhere I go."

I watch as she runs to one corner of the yard as calls out, "See? He's following me!"

I'm entranced as she frolics to the opposite corner of the yard, spinning around as if catching the moon in the act of chasing her. "See!? He's STILL there!" She giggles recklessly.

I smile realizing that the moon does appear to follow as we move about, completely loyal and unquestioning, quietly observing. Taking in the wisdom of this tiny girl. I step off the porch and follow her lead. She is my world after all.

"That's right baby girl, you ARE the leader of the moon."

~K.G. Carroll ~

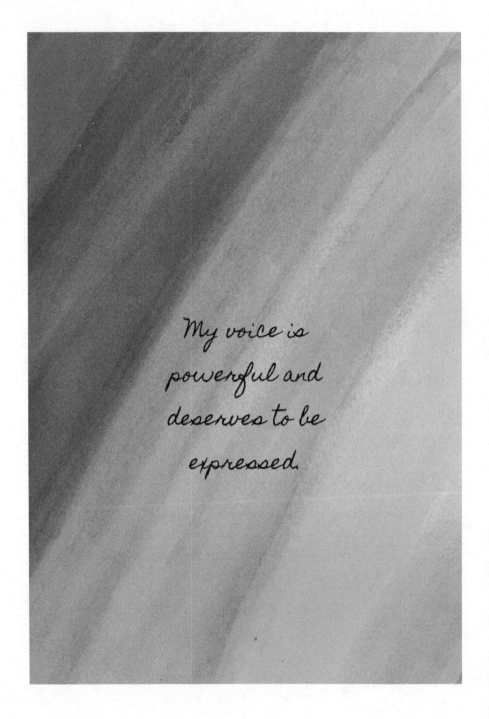

My voice is powerful and deserves to be expressed.

The Messy Parts

The years they change us
Some good, some bad
Make proud who raised us
Mom & Dad

Speak up or stay quiet
Choices to choose
Conversation may strain us
Each side may lose

Respect your elders
They know what's right
But why do they lie
When they can no longer fight

Is it fair to shield emotions
Is it fair to hide the truth
Why must pride get in the way
Why must every question be removed

Whether truth or lie from lips brings
We are stronger than you think
Remember at the end
The pain of a loss still stings

~James Wesley

The Messy Parts

Her Story

My three children are all very different from each other. My oldest, born at the end of a seven year relationship with his father, was a brilliant child. I don't mean, in a "My child is the smartest", proud mom way. He was speaking in complete sentences by the time he was eighteen months old. He was reading on his own, at age three. In most social settings, he preferred making conversation with the adults in the room, to any activity with his peers. When his name was not selected in the "Pre-K Lottery" for a spot in our district Pre-K program, I was told to bring him to the school for an evaluation that might offer him a placement in the "Eagle" (gifted) program. Of course, he was accepted into the program. Toward the end of that school year, I was asked to sign a permission letter, to have him evaluated for the "super duper gifted" program, known as CIG, (Children who are Intellectually Gifted). Again, he scored incredibly and was offered one of twenty-eight placements, for which sixteen hundred students had been "tested". He attended the program, (to which he was bussed, outside our district), through kindergarten and half of first grade. By the middle of the second term in the program, I realized, the workload the program was putting on six year old kids was beyond any sense of reason, I could wrap my head around. Three hours of homework in first grade seemed excessive to me. He wasn't struggling with the work. There was, legitimately, three hours of work. His math homework included the use of Cuisenaire rods, for geometry problems. It was 1996, and I was thirty-two years old, and I had never heard of Cuisenaire rods. I couldn't rationalize the idea of putting my kid through six hours of work in school, another three hours of work at home, and no time left for just being a kid, so I pulled him out of the program.

For the next few years, he thrived, academically. He remained in the district "gifted" program, through fifth grade. While his grades and test scores remained high, he encountered difficulties in socialization and with "following the rules". He questioned EVERYTHING, much to my "proud mom" delight, and my "concerned mom" dismay. How much trouble he created for himself always seemed to depend on the response of the teacher, at the time. His second grade teacher would allow him to wander around the classroom, to utilize the reading, or creativity centers once he finished his work. She felt it was a reward for completing his work quickly, and it was a way to keep him out of trouble because he was bored, waiting for the rest of the class to finish. His fourth grade teacher did not find his quick completion of classwork and subsequent fidgeting to be "reward worthy". Instead, she was constantly yelling. "Sit still." "Stop tapping your pencil." "Stop whistling." "No, you may not go to the bathroom." She sent home note, after note, telling me about "behavior problems". During parent-teacher conferences, she told me he should be evaluated and possibly medicated. She recommended a psychiatrist. I was never one of those "Not MY child" kind of moms. I considered everything the teacher had said, weighed it against every other difficulty my son seemed to be facing, and I scheduled an appointment to see the doctor.

That first psychiatrist was very rigid. She was older, and seemed to come from a very "children should be seen, and not heard" perspective. After only two or three sessions with my son, the doctor was breaking out her prescription pad, and recommending Ritalin. I had found out that this doctor was a friend of the fourth grade teacher. I also found out, through conversations with some of the other parents, about a third of the class was taking Ritalin. None of it sat right with me, so I respectfully declined the prescription, and canceled all future appointments. I wasn't denying the idea that my son might need some help. I was simply not comfortable with the idea that after three forty-five minute sessions, this "professional" had determined that my kid needed to be medicated. Medication can be a life saving therapy, but in my opinion, it should not be the first option, ESPECIALLY in children.

I researched additional therapy options. We didn't have the best insurance at the time, so I made an appointment with a PSYCHOLOGIST, (who provide therapy, WITHOUT prescriptions), through a church program. The available psychologist seemed as if she may have been a nun, at some point, and I half expected her to slap my hand with a ruler, if I didn't answer her questions correctly. After spending a few sessions with my son, she told me she believed my kid was exhibiting symptoms of ODD, (Oppositional Defiant Disorder). He had no respect for authority, she said. He argued against everything she told him and refused to comply, when she gave him instructions. She believed he should be in intensive therapy, and might benefit from medication. As I left the office, she gave me one of those judgmental glares that told me she thought I was just another hippy mother, in denial. I WAS in denial. I was denying a medical and education system that promotes blindly medicating children, to make them easily compliant. Nope.

I found another psychologist, who was highly recommended by other parents. Please keep in mind, this was 1999. Google was only a year old, and certainly wasn't accessible in everyone's pocket, just yet. It was not my intention to discuss my (then) nine-year-old son's challenges with the neighborhood, but my kid needed help, so I reached out to a few friends, and they reached out to their friends. The new doctor was a man in his forties, and my kid seemed more comfortable with this doctor. We continued seeing him for as many sessions as our insurance would cover. After four or five visits, I asked the doctor if he thought my son needed additional help. "He is a very smart, well adjusted young man. I don't see any need for additional therapy." My first thought was, "Well, he's got YOUR number". I thanked the doctor for his assessment and realized there would be no trustworthy, reliable help for my kid, and it was all on me to help him navigate any challenge he might face.

Around this time, I was in the midst of planning a wedding. We had been together for almost seven years, and living as a family for five of those years. We had been through some challenging periods. The stepfather/stepchild dynamic was tense, at times. Ultimately, I was madly in love and building a better life for me and my kid. I wanted more children. I did everything I had to do, to keep peace, which often included keeping my kid quiet. I often failed at that task, which led to more tension. It was a constant balancing act, trying to keep everyone happy, but we managed to make it work, however dysfunctionally it was working.

Less than a year after the wedding, we welcomed my second child. It was very clear that my new husband resented the fact that his firstborn child was not MY firstborn child. When our new baby came down with RSV at four weeks old, my husband blamed my oldest for bringing home the germ that hospitalized our new son. The resentment was festering. The joy my oldest son felt in his new role as a big brother was poisoned by my husband's resentment. I did my best to encourage the bonding between my children, while trying to shield my oldest from comments like, "Could you tell your kid to stop touching the baby's hands?" He then rarely called my son by his name. Despite my constant insistence that my child deserved to be called by his name, my increasingly angry husband only referred to my oldest as "your kid", which led to "my kid" growing increasingly angry. The balancing act of keeping the peace had become a unicycle ride across a tightrope.

The first few months with the new baby were challenging. He was colicky for four months, barely sleeping. My husband was working on a construction project that required him to be at work for quite a few sixteen hour days, so it was all on me to handle an all night crying baby, so that daddy could get some sleep. "You can nap during the day", I was told. But the baby cried all day, too. We tried breastfeeding, this formula, that formula, and nothing helped. The doctor said he was healthy and that some babies just cry. I don't know if we finally struck on the right formula, or if a miracle finally found its way to my little guy, but after that four months, the crying just stopped. He still didn't sleep well, but I thanked all the gods for a suddenly content baby. It finally seemed like we could have what resembled a "normal" family life.

When the baby was about a year old, I started to notice development issues that led me to seek out some input from the pediatrician. He was walking and babbling, as babies do, but there were little things that felt...off. "Doctor, when I ask the baby, 'Where's Daddy', shouldn't he be looking around the room?" The doctor seemed unconcerned. "All babies develop at their own pace. Give him six months and we'll see how it goes." Six months later, I told the doctor, "He seems to ignore me when I call his name. I don't think his hearing is a problem, because if he hears Barney come on the television, he comes running from the other side of the house. Should I be concerned?" The doctor still seemed to have no worries about what I saw as delays or deficits in development, but he said, "If you want to put your mind at ease, you can make an appointment to have him evaluated." That was it. He didn't say WHERE I could have my child evaluated, or by whom. Just a big "don't worry" smile. Around the same time, my sister-in-law called me and said, "Don't get mad, but I was looking up symptoms of autism and I think you might want to have the baby checked out". As human nature dictates, I was annoyed that my in-laws felt the need to step into a concern I was already addressing, but I recognized their concern was coming from a place of love. After talking to some friends in the medical and educational fields, I made an appointment to have my son evaluated. On his second birthday, my son was diagnosed with autism. And I was three months pregnant with my third child.

The tightrope of my balancing act was now on fire.

I have always been a "glass half full" kind of person. My husband was NOT. I jumped into obtaining support with both feet. No sadness, no anger, full speed ahead. No one could tell me how profoundly my child would be affected by the diagnosis, and all I wanted to do was to give him every opportunity to grow and develop to whatever potential he could. My husband couldn't see the path forward quite so clearly. He was angry. He cursed God and the universe. The resentment he felt for my older son had become a seething hatred. Why did this happen to HIS son and not to my oldest? He had followed all the rules in life and did everything that was expected of him, so why was he being "punished"? It took us a long time to get past that initial anger and self pity party. Eventually, he came around and our life became consumed with all things autism. After that, any small peeks of love or compassion he may ever have shown to my oldest were gone. Any time he looked at my firstborn, all he saw was "NOT autistic". For my sake, he tried to be...civilized, but his resentment seeped into any interaction between them. And just to make matters as complicated as they could possibly be, my oldest was in the throes of puberty. The flaming tightrope was dipped in gasoline.

After a particularly heated confrontation between my husband and my oldest, we all decided it might be best if my son went to live with his dad for a while. I wasn't trying to simplify my own life. I was trying to protect my son from the toxicity of the resentment of my husband. With every new challenge my middle child faced, and with a new baby girl in the house, I had to give my oldest an opportunity to escape a burden that was not his to carry. I spoke to him regularly. He would call me to tell me his stepmother wasn't clean. He would take a dish out of the cabinet and it would be greasy, with bits of food still on it. I told him he could help out by washing the dishes himself. He didn't call to tell me he wanted to come home. I think our house no longer felt like "home" to him. But I know he missed being with me, so he would call to tell me little things that might make me want to "rescue" him. After five weeks, his stepmother called me to tell me he was cutting up the pillows in his room with a steak knife, and it might be best if he came back to live with me. It was a rough transition, and we established some rules and some boundaries to keep peace in the house, but at the time, I think my husband and my son loved me enough to make an effort to get along. Some people might question why I would stay with a man who made life so uncomfortable for my oldest child. I questioned it myself. But I loved them both. I was also managing school and doctors and therapy for a newly diagnosed toddler, and caring for an infant daughter. I was a stay at home mom, with no real prospects to make a sustainable living on my own. Where was I going? So I stayed and did the best I could to make sure everyone in the house was loved and cared for. It was all I could do.

The next few years were challenging. My middle child hardly slept, the baby was also not a good sleeper, and all of this meant that I was barely getting any sleep. I was tired, constantly running from one therapy appointment to another. My oldest was pushing the envelope of teen rebellion to the very edge of its breaking point. He no longer cared about his grades, or school. He had some friends, and thankfully managed to stay out of any real trouble, but certainly found every way possible, (within the confines of the law), to act out his frustration at a complicated life in which he felt trapped. When he was about fourteen years old, we had the "coming out" conversation. I initiated the conversation. I knew he was gay when he was two years old. It never mattered to me, but my son needed to know, beyond a shadow of a doubt, that I loved him exactly as he was. Talking about it seemed to provide him with some relief. I had hoped that by getting his "secret" out in the open, he might feel more at ease and less angry. There was a more relaxed bond between me and my son, but his anger didn't waiver. The anger was never about me.

We might've spent the next few years in a "walking on eggshells" existence, but we were all consumed with all things "autism". There was no room for what (to me, at the time) seemed like petty shit. I was trying to be a good mother and a good wife, and to just make an attempt at creating a happy life for all of us. I did my best to be a peacekeeper and spread myself thin to make sure everyone had what they needed. In doing so, I was failing miserably, but in the moment, we were getting by. Fortunately, even in the absence of a decent sleep schedule, my daughter added only joy to the mix. She was a happy baby. Like her oldest brother, she was speaking in complete sentences by eighteen months and she was smart as a whip. Before she was two, she was helping to take care of her brother. She would run to bring me diapers, or to bring her brother a juicebox. She would watch videos with him and come to tell me if he needed something. She was sweet and thoughtful and polite and loving. It felt like the universe knew I needed a break, and she was, for the most part, the easiest, most people pleasing child I had ever known. She absolutely adored both of her brothers and she was her daddy's princess. All of the anger my husband felt toward God and the universe disappeared when he looked at his little girl. He showered her with love and anything she could possibly want. The more he loved her, the more my oldest felt UNloved.

My oldest was not an easy child. He was too smart for his own good, right from the beginning. But he wasn't a "bad" kid. I don't think he ever understood what he could possibly have done to make my husband "hate" him, the way he felt he did. The psychological depth of what had created the wall between them was far too complicated for a teenage boy to comprehend. Whatever deep mental "reasons" my husband had for carrying an undeserved resentment, there was no excuse. There is no acceptable reason a grown man should hold a child "responsible" for what he perceived to be his own "misfortune", but there we all were. I couldn't change who my husband was. I could only try to love all of my family, in the way they each needed to be loved. I tried, but the needs of my middle child held a great deal of my time and attention. By the time my oldest was almost seventeen, he started asking to sleep at a friend's house. Two, three nights in a row, then a week would go by. I let him stay, because it saved him from what he was feeling at home. After the second week, I asked him if he was ever coming home. He said, "Mom, I can't be there anymore". As much as my mama heart was broken, I let him go. The friend lived with her mom and a few other stray teens, who had come from challenging homes. I stayed in contact with him, saw him regularly, made sure he had everything he needed, and I let him go.

My oldest is now almost thirty-three years old. He is successfully running his own business and is in a relationship that makes him happy. We have had lots of conversations over the years about all of the choices I made that hurt him. He has reminded me of some of those poor choices and the way he felt, going through it all as a child. I have apologized to him many times for all the things I should've done differently. Every time, he tells me I don't have to be sorry. He tells me he appreciates the apology, but doesn't need it. He tells me that by acknowledging my responsibility in the ways he was damaged, he is able to forgive me for all of it. He feels validated. He feels heard. He's not angry. He's grateful. He tells me, every choice I made, even the ones that hurt him the most, made him stronger. He tells me, even as a child, he knew I was doing the best I could. He knew I was trying to give him a better life and that everything I did was out of love. He tells me he wished I could have left my husband, not for him, but for me. Eventually, he got his wish. It may seem as if the wish came true too late for my son to benefit from the freedom of removing the toxic presence from my life, but that is not true. I am an infinitely better version of myself, now that I no longer feel the need to be what someone else needs me to be. I can look back and own responsibility for the damage my choices have caused, and I can take comfort in knowing I have become a better mother and a better person. I don't feel guilty. Guilt is too heavy a burden to bear. I am simply grateful to have learned from my mistakes. I'm grateful that no matter what we went through, my kids have always known they were loved. I'm grateful for the deeply close relationships I have with my (now) grown children. I'm grateful for the kind, loving, intelligent, polite, considerate, strong, independent people my kids have grown to be, because of, and in spite of the way I raised them. I am grateful for everything they have taught me along the way, and for everything they continue to teach me. I am grateful for their open minds, and for their desire to always know more and to do better. There are plenty of ways I have broken my kids, but there has always been enough love to mend what was broken and to build an unbreakable bond between us.

~Donna Blasi Miglino

Painting by Wendy Tobin

The burden falls to the mother.

I didn't ask to be in constant over function, but here I am. I do the laundry, wash the dishes, keep track of medicines, appointment a, diagnosis, IEP's. I manage the meltdowns and the groceries. I make pop tarts for lunch because I'm too sick to stand. But the guilt is stronger than the nausea so I run laps between the toilet and the stove, raw hands from constant washing. I feel invisible yet touched out. I want to scream if I have to hold one more thing yet here you are, cuddled into my shoulder. I keep a box of dreams in the back of the closet. My "one days, some days, and maybe's" collecting dust while I make cupcakes you won't eat because they are the wrong color.

I am lonely but never alone. Never the chance to breathe because that would take too much time.

I didn't get to brush my teeth but damn does your smile sparkle.

~Lola Lawrence~

An Adieu to Motherhood

I feel a constant pain in my stomach.

Why am I now restricted to abort
When both of our lives are in danger?

I am losing my baby
And my baby is losing his mother either way,
This is our heart wrenching life,
Cohabitating in the same body.

Why should I be the one
To be lawfully condemned!

What decision will we have
Other than death?

Losing a combat against humanity
Is already a lost love,
Now losing a baby is a pierced heartbreak.

~Alshaad Kara~

Suffering in the Silence

Suffering and struggling in silence. That is how I felt sometimes. Alone, confused, and desperate for answers. Actually, I wasn't the silent one... at all. I felt like I was screaming and hollering and even begging at times. Silence was the response I received. I was constantly asking the pediatrician why certain behaviors were happening, and why certain others were not. I continually asked friends and family members about their experiences with their children's development. I was always asking other parents and teachers for advice. Really took notice of other children's "normal" and "typical" age appropriate development. Ignoring the voices in my head telling me something wasn't right. Completely over thinking every parenting decision I made. I made lists of odd and questionable behaviors, talked with my husband in circles until I couldn't even form another logical thought. Hoping my natural parenting instincts are wrong, but then realizing that whether they were or not, I needed help. I was trying to balance common sense with all the early childhood education I learned in college. Researching and reading everything I could on positive discipline, good parenting strategies, helpful hints on raising good children, and praying. I prayed like my life (and sanity) depended on it, because... actually it did. And so did my daughter's. I was her voice, her advocate at that crucial stage in her three and a half year old life. If I didn't fight for her, who would? I was searching tirelessly for answers when no one believed there was even a problem.

I am beyond grateful that God chose me to be this very special little girl's mom. Some days I am on the brink of losing my sanity as well as my patience, but I am learning more and more every day. I am not perfect, but I am doing my very best. I am trying to see the world through Madison's magnified senses and view the natural beauty that is within her grasp. She really is amazing and has taught me so much about life, love, and myself. I am forever grateful for the opportunity to be a better mom and a better person through what she is teaching me.

~Samantha Woodbeck

I sketched that picture and wrote those words in a personal blog post in 2013, on the brink of my daughter's Autism diagnosis.

The Messy Parts

In Your Honour

It's your birthday today and I miss you.

How am I meant to live with such pain?

Though my soul knows that you are a part of me still

and hopes one day to see you again.

Some days the burden's just too heavy

my heart cannot carry its weight.

Somehow I push forward without you

my perpetual grief now innate.

It's your birthday today and I miss you,

although years have flown by since you left.

Time cannot heal a wound such as this

part of me is forever bereft.

My head knows that you'd be all grown now

maybe you'd be a mum by now too,

yet I picture you still as my baby

like you were the last time I held you.

It's your birthday today and I miss you,

think I'll miss you until my last breath.

I sometimes close my eyes

Think I feel you;

Our bond so strong even in death.

There are times when I think I can't bear it,

this missing you year after year.

But I live every day for you angel,

through the sorrow, the smiles, the tears.

Try to see the whole world through your young eyes;

Full of wonder and childlike glee,

taking every breath in your honour

holding tightly to your memory.

~Brenda Cierniak~

A Mothers Love

Tough love
Melt down number 54
Loudly and ferociously you Roar
Another new hole in the kitchen door
Yet still I look; and can only love you more.

An endless round of verbal abuse
The harshest of words you find and use
Flying fists and flying shoes
Yet still Its unconditional love I choose

The tears of frustration flow fiercely again
Bearing every past trauma and all the pain
The sensory overload of your growing brain
Yet only love for you remains.

The anger and rage you birth into being
The ways in which you are acting and perceiving
The violence, hate and hurt we are feeling
And still through eyes of love I am seeing.

A Mother's Love
Can be cruel and tough.
A constant questioning of am I good enough?
Yet always we manage to still find that love.

~Samantha Young

My Purpose

So… growing up I struggled. I had a writing disability and struggled with my weight. My dad was an alcoholic and my parents struggled financially and emotionally. I was never proud of anything. I was clumsy as hell. My dad often told me I could hardly walk and chew bubble gum... I barely passed every year in school. I had friends but was not the popular kid at all....My life was ok.

Until April 10 2002. I gave birth to a beautiful baby girl. I will never forget that moment when she took her first breath. I had a PURPOSE. It was the PROUDEST MOMENT of my life. She was all mine. I did something AMAZING...

I had my second daughter on June 1st 2005. The second most AMAZING DAY of my LIFE.

I had my 3rd daughter on February 24 2008. The third most AMAZING DAY of my LIFE.

My girls are my EVERYTHING. I see the best of me in all of them. It isn't always perfect and there have been many tears throughout this last 21 years. I am thankful for each of my BEAUTIES for giving me a PURPOSE: MARTINA, BELLA, AND AUNAH'S MOMMA...

~Teresa Price~

The Price

As any parent who loves their child knows,

You pay a price to the gods

The very moment that they are placed within your arms.

You are sentenced to a lifetime of worry and heartache,

Wondering if you'll be able to give them enough,

Keep them safe enough,

Prepare them enough,

Love them enough…

If you are enough.

The ironic part about it all

Is no matter how old they get,

They will always look at you like you're a superhero,

The very force that holds their universe together.

Remember,

To them, you are more than enough –

You are everything.

~Charlene Ann Benoit

If I had One Wish

If I had one wish in my life
it would be for you
to see yourself through my eyes
You would see an overwhelming love
an admiration of who you are becoming
You would see my heart and soul
being proud of you
and the strength you are developing
deep in your soul
Please always remember
to keep your heart open
no matter what
Never stop laughing
because your laughter is contagious
Love like it could be your last day
Never be sorry for who you are
Live life to the fullest
Dance to music you hear
even if nobody else hears it
Always stay kind to others,
feel things deeply and have no regrets
I love you with all my heart
and will always be proud of
the person you are
and who you truly aspire to be

~Tegan Matthews, TGN Poetry~

Photograph credit: Swiger Photography, Philadelphia PA

Tegan Matthews, TGN Poetry

When They Were Born

The drowning love and maternal bursts of air through my lungs almost drove me

mad in a love song, evermore, forever sort of way.

She is my first born; dragon eyes, bouncy curls, full of wonder and fire

and sassy swirls.

A heart shimmering in amethyst and a soul of wild delight, my mini me;

the best of me, strong and carefree

beautiful as the full moon on a dark, Autumn night.

You completed the woman that I came to be

the brightest star in all the land from enchanted forest to majestic sea.

He is my second born, a gorgeous boy that crowned my love

all sage and storms, snuggles and hugs.

He is a different version of me, wild and gentle, loves to be close, but

longs to be free.

Beautiful as the sun on a bright summer's day

a love like no other in that mother and son sort of way.

He gleams like the moon in all the sky

the keeper of my heart, the apple of my eye.

~Ann Marie Eleazer~

The Messy Parts

I'll always be your shoulder

in any time of need;

I'd move the tallest mountains

if it meant that you'd succeed.

I promise to be your shelter

against any torrential rains.

My heart is yours forever;

its blood runs through your veins.

I'll keep your spaces softened,

furnished for any landing.

While my heart provides pure warmth,

prepared for understanding.

Nothing will ever compare to

this love I feel in my heart;

I will be your beacon of strength

until death will have us part.

~T.B. Elden~

More Than Words

From the moment you were born
I was forever changed.
You stole my heart
my soul, you rearranged.

You opened my eyes
to things I didn't even know.
I discovered life all over again
as I constantly watched you grow.

I love you fiercely,
all the fears mixed with wonder,
So much to learn,
for both of us to discover.

I'm beyond grateful to be your mom,
you bless me every single day.
You mean so much to me,
Even more than these words could ever say.

~Samantha Woodbeck

The Messy Parts

Unconventional perfection
Stymied in a world
That only celebrates narrow minded drones
Misunderstood
White coats flapped incessantly
Saying we had to change you
Forced conforming
Into boxes not made for you
Diminish your beauty
Break the bones of uniqueness
Until you lay inside their design
Steal your humanity
Until you were paint by numbers perfect
I said no…
They don't see you as I see you
They don't know you as I know you
I fell in love with the view in your eyes
Finding new wonders to marvel
Amazed at the intricate turning
Of the cogs and wheels of your mind
Making nonsense logical
And sense gibberish
I see you
I hear you
Even when the world
Is trapped between your teeth.

~Lola Lawrence~

Unspoken

You catch me looking at photos of you

From nearly a decade ago,

Longing for moments when

You needed me more.

You wrap your arms around my waist,

Bury your head into my shoulder –

The unspoken promise

That you'll always be

My baby.

~Charlene Ann Benoit

A Mother From a Child's Eyes

A Mother.
When you hear the word
"Mother,"
Do you think
Of a single thing
That is negative?
Because I don't.
Because when I think of a mother
I think of someone
That would go to the ends of the earth
To protect you.
Someone
Who would always be there
No matter what
Someone who has sacrificed
So much just
To see you smile.
This beautiful person
Inside and out
That created you.
That went through so much
To give you life.
Because when I think of a mother
I think of a person that will love me for who I am
No matter what.
Through rain and shine.
So if someone in this world
Can call you
"Mother"
I think
That is one of the greatest achievements in life
That you can receive.

~Dani Majestic, Age 11~

Addison
(Oh Christmas Tree melody)

Oh Addison, Oh Addison
Oh how I love my Addison.
From fingertips to rosebud lips,
Those tiny toes, and button nose,

Oh Addison, Oh Addison
Oh how I love my Addison.
Cute little ears, and grumpy sneers.
Deep blue eyes and sleepy sighs,

Oh Addison, Oh Addison
Oh how I love my Addison.
If you only knew, how much I love you,
I think you'd let, your mommy rest,

BUT...

Oh Addison, Oh Addison
Oh how I love my Addison.
I'll carry you, all night through.
I'll keep you safe, in my embrace.

Oh Addison, Oh Addison
Oh how I love my Addison.
I'll be here, to ease your fears.
You can believe that I'll never leave.

Oh Addison, Oh Addison
Oh how I love my Addison.

~K.G. Carroll~

My Sweet Boy

He is kind
He is strong
He loves without reservation
His soft little heart
Is mine in duplication

He's courageous and smart
Even argues that he doesn't like art

Even though he was carved
From the same spirit as my very own heart
He can't see it now, but he will in time
I see depth in his soul
That will carry him through
This life and others…
The will of the creator,
And the mission he is meant to do.

To Hudson
with love,
Mom

~Samantha Woodbeck

Photo by Nicole Cotta Photography

When a Mama fights for her kids, she will do everything that needs to be done to protect them. She will sacrifice her life for her babies. Her childhood dreams are put to the side to nurture her children's dreams. In a mother's world, time stands still in the smallest moments, and whizzes by as she sees her little ones become themselves. The most terrible pain a mom feels is knowing she can never protect her kids from the suffering parts of life. She wishes only to cradle them under her shield, however; she knows they need the struggle in order to become their best selves. There is a bond that we all have with our mother that ties us back to the tick of her heartbeat, the steady in her breath, the song of her voice. Mama knows she's not perfect, but in her eyes, she created perfection in her womb.

~Anonymous~

Out of the Mouths of Babes

My 8 year old boy asked me a question about an age restricted video game.

He said "Why do you have to be 18 to play Grand Theft Auto but you can join the army at 16?"

I replied saying "because there's a lot of swearing in the game."

His response: "and there's a lot of dying in the army."

Early morning childhood musings!

~Danielle Gibbens

The Messy Parts

There are many types of love in this world,
but the strongest love of all,
By far,
Is the love from a mother.
The heart of our home,
the bones of our family.
Of all the ways to describe a mother's love,
the most accurate might be
"relentless."
It overcomes all,
the greatest sacrifices
and the most thankless of jobs.
So,
thank you.
Thank you for the greatest gift you
could have ever given.
For enduring, for fighting,
for guiding hands that seem to know
exactly when to push us to become more,
and when to pull us in and hold us close.
Whatever becomes of me, know how
much is owed to you,
your love.
Wherever I may wander to,
know that you are my home,
my heart,
my bones.
I'll grow, I'll make us proud,
and when you look in my eyes, I hope
you can see yourself.
You see the parts of you instilled
in me,
burning brightly, and being shared,
relentlessly.

~J. Raymond

LAYNE ISAAC

The day that you were born we knew that

God had plans

We wouldn't get to have you long or hold your tiny hands

To watch you grow, to laugh or play

To grow to be a man

All because God needed you

It was his heavenly plan.

It broke our hearts to let you go

To try to understand

But having faith in God above and trusting in His plan.

The pain of losing you that day will never ever fade

You were so sweet and innocent.

So perfectly made.

For my grandson, Layne

With so much love,

~Stacey Miller-Sommerfeld

The Messy Parts

Diane's Little Reminders…
On Being a Mother

1. A child is born without baggage. Don't give them yours, like guilt, shame, fear or blame.
2. Never be their critic, just their praise and encouragement.
3. May the memory of your hand upon their face always be a sense of love and comfort, not an angry sting.
4. Never let them fall asleep crying alone. Be their comfort no matter how old they are.
5. Please don't yell and scream at them. Be their source of peace, not anxiety.
6. Tell them stories and read to them. Don't make TV their source of learning.
7. Let them walk barefoot on your lawn as the rain falls.
8. Let them smell real food cooking in the kitchen when they come home, not a microwave meal.
9. Teach them about God to the best of your understanding. Theres nothing wrong in going to Sunday school.
10. Don't force them to eat food they don't like.
11. Teach them to say "Please" and "Thank you." "Sorry" and "Excuse me."
12. Allow them to believe in Santa Clause and Fairy Godmothers. Childhood fantasies are so short lived.
13. Never be their source of pain.
14. Tell them you love them everyday, if possible. Hug them and touch them often.
15. Teach them how to be creative; to draw, to color, write and paint.
16. Don't let your child cover their ears and say, "Mommy, please don't scream."
17. There's no retirement age for being a mother. It's a lifetime position.

18. If a child is afraid of the dark, leave a light on for them, instead of yelling, "There's nothing to be afraid of."
19. Give them small chores. Make them responsible for something.
20. Don't be afraid, or feel guilty in saying the word "No." Start very early in saying it.
21. Too many broken promises will affect their trust in you.
22. Teach them how to cook and clean. To be amazed at butterflies, insects, sunsets and thunderstorms.
23. A child is like a piece of clay. You are the potter. Mold them well.
24. What you show and teach your child in the first few years of life will last a lifetime.
25. As a mother you have the greatest responsibility of anyone on Earth. Make it a beautiful journey for your child and yourself.

In closing:

Yes, it will be difficult, overwhelming, exhausting, and very demanding.

Such is the joy and plight of motherhood. I am the mother of four adult children who love and respect me today as they did as children.

No, I wasn't perfect, but I did raise them with all the "Little Reminders" I've written for you.

~Diane McLaughlin~

Things our mom always said growing up…

"Dynamite comes in small packages."

"Beggars can't be choosers."

"Nice to meet you, Hungry/Bored. I'm Mom!"

"Improvise, adapt, and overcome."

"I'd rather be pissed off than pissed on."

Me: "Hey mom, how are you?"
Mom: "Just ducky, thanks!"

"Peachy keen, jelly bean."

"Hot diggity dog."

"Sounds like a plan, Stan!"

"Great minds think alike."

"Good genes run in the family."

Any compliment ever: "You get it from your mom."

~Samantha Woodbeck and siblings;
Robyn Majestic, Steven Robinson, and Candis Gurzenski

The Messy Parts

About our amazing contributors…

Nicole Dax is a caregiver to Mom throughout her cancer journey, and her Grandmother's right arm during her later years of life. Managed by a funny little dog, and a lot of coffee.

Samantha's note: (because she'll never give herself enough credit for all she has done and continues to do). On top of being an extremely talented writer and caregiver, Nicole is an amazing advocate for mental health awareness and is the most selfless human I know. She has encouraged, motivated, and pushed me out of my comfort zone as a writer in more ways than I can say. She was instrumental in putting this special anthology together by recruiting other writers and giving endless support and energy on our social media posts. One day she and I will meet for coffee and talk, cry, and laugh until we lose our voices. This book wouldn't be what it is without her unwavering support. I am thankful and beyond blessed to call her a friend. You can find her on social media @ By Daxology

The Messy Parts

Introducing myself, I would first like to say, I am very excited to be a part of this group. Thank you very much for giving me the opportunity to offer my creative input to such a wonderful cause. Motherhood is the hardest job in this world. I feel that in order to be a great mother, I need to be the best version of myself. That is always a work in progress. As I am raising my children throughout their entire lives, they get to see me through many stages of struggles, losses, gains and growth. The lessons I teach them impact their lives in so many ways. I only pray they gain strength through me to handle whatever comes their way in life.

My name is **Mary Klaisner**. I am a retired Media Instructional Paraeducator. I am in search of my second career in life. In between job searching, I have tapped into my creative side, creating my Just. Be. Facebook Page.

I have been writing all my life. I have an online platform that is for self publishing where I have been compiling poems for years. I have dreamed of publishing a poetry book at some time in my life. Tomorrows aren't promised so when I was inspired by other Poetry Pages, I decided to move forward with Just. Be. and get my poems out there.I hope to touch the lives of others through my expressive words. Poetry has been a tool for my growth as a person. It releases emotions that are buried in my soul that need to be freed so I can move forward.

In connecting with The Messy Parts Anthology FaceBook group of writers, I look forward to growing through so many other talented writers.

The Messy Parts

Photograph credit: Swiger Photography, Philadelphia PA

Tegan Matthews
(TGN Poetry, the gorgeous nothing)

I am a poet and writer. Throughout my life, I often felt like an impostor. I began writing poetry about love, loss, regret, trials, and tribulations along the way to process decisions I made and my actions.

Recently, I have been writing erotic poetry, short stories, and working on my first fiction novel. Living right outside Philadelphia my whole life, I've had many city adventures to include and not so city adventures. The majority of my writings are about small moments that have taken place throughout my life and accepting, coming to terms with who I am ~ my evolution as you will. My writing is also focused on capturing memories I have experienced that pushed me and developed who I am today mixed with a little bit of fiction and of course with flair and excitement. The poems included in this anthology are dedicated to three of my children, who are my life and my reason.

Jenna Dixon is a special needs mom who lives in the mountains of South Central Pennsylvania with her partner and their two children. She is passionate about nature and is currently studying Environmental Science so she can be more involved with the natural environment around her. Jenna has had a passion for writing from a young age. As a domestic violence survivor she took her passion for writing and started an online community where she shares her writing in hopes of fostering an atmosphere of healing, growth and empowerment. You can find her work on Facebook at Ramblings of a Beautiful Bohemian Soul.

Charlene Ann Benoit was born and raised in Newfoundland, Canada. She began writing poetry at age ten, and in 2004, she finished her first collection, *Pieces of My Soul*. In 2005, she completed her first novel, *When Walls Come Crashing Down*. Since that time, she has completed eight other books of poetry, *In Memory Of* (2005), *Shattered* (2008), *Between the Lines* (2019), *In the Hearts of Gods, Monsters, and Men* (2020), *Blood, Tears and Coffee Rings* (2020), *Fairy Tales & Other Things I Tell Myself* (2021), *The Road That Led Me Nowhere* (2021), and *Finding Redemption* (2022. She has also written a children's book, *The Littlest Prince* (2015), which is awaiting illustrations, and a novella called *Death's Daughter* (2018). She has also been included in various anthologies.

Currently, she has several other projects in the works, including her upcoming novels, *The Skeptic*, and *Whispers from Neverland*
You can find more of her writing on Facebook and Instagram:

https://www.facebook.com/themidnightmoth
https://www.instagram.com/themidnightmoth/

She can be reached at:
midnightmothpublicationsinc@gmail.com

Alshaad Kara is a Mauritian poet who writes from his heart. His latest poems were published in one anthology, "Gal's Guide Anthology: Journey", two magazines, "100subtexts issue 7" and "Prodigy Magazine-February 2023" and two journals, "Orion's Beau Winter 2023: A Love Worth Losing" and "Literary Cognizance Vol.- III, Issue-4, March 2023".

My name is **Jessica Wateski**. I'm from Pittston, PA. I'm a 36 year old mom of two wonderful kids. Son, Caleb, age 13; daughter, Payton, age 9. Both children are the reason I'm still here today. I have been writing since I was 9 or 10. It is my mental therapy release. It has been my dream to get published somewhere, anywhere just to get my name and feelings about life's journey out there.

The Messy Parts

They say to be a poet you need to experience either love or heartbreak. I say to be a poet you need to really just experience life! As life is a journey full of moments just waiting to be captured.

Purpleprincessness was born as a consequence of a need to express everyday raw emotions that not everyone talks about. To find words that visualize sentiment with ardour. In my opinion I'm a writer of simple raw relatable vehemence.

My anonymity gives me the freedom to be enigmatic, like wearing an invisibility cloak whilst absorbing my surroundings and using words to convey fervour.

I love to express myself using different forms of poetry and prose and my preferred genre being love. Love poetry has become a trademark for me and it gives me great pleasure to help others express this wonderful emotion/feeling.

A friend recognised in me talent which I still struggle to see at times but feel grateful to have found my poetic voice. As any writer finding people resonating is the biggest appreciation for our art. It not only empowers but gives us motivation to continue.

I'm available on the following social media platforms:

FB: https://www.facebook.com/purpleprincessness?mibextid=ZbWKwL
IG: https://instagram.com/purpleprincessness?igshid=ZDdkNTZiNTM=

Ann Marie Eleazer's poetry will take you on an enchanted flight through magical places she's been drawn to since childhood.

What started out as a creative outlet soon became an unleashing of what lies beneath into her world of fairytale darkness and poetic passion.

She began sharing her work in 2017 on a variety of social media platforms and the desire to publish her work grew.

A lover of all things ancient, haunted and otherworldly, Ann Marie enjoys collecting books, filling pages with magic and spending time in her home with her family and furbabies.

The Messy Parts

Mary-Kate is a Celtic writer and poet. She is a happily married mommy of four little ones. MK was born in Scotland and raised in Ireland on the West coast of County Mayo in Crossmolina with her Irish parents.

MK began writing again after her mum: Lily died suddenly in 2013. Her books were published to give her dad: Tommy some hope, but he passed away in 2018 after many strokes.

MK has a teaching PGCE and a Broadcasting Degree. She has worked as a TV Camerawoman for over 20 years. She has retrained as a celebrant which she does alongside being a mommy, a television camerawoman, a teacher, a lecturer, a writer, and a poet. She now lives in South Devon, England.

She has written two poetry books (Love Life Poetry: A Dreamer of Improbable Dreams and Love Life Poetry: Staring at the Stars) as well as a children's book (Lily the Leprechaun and the Wailing Banshee) All her books are available to buy on Amazon.

@lovelifepoetry by MK AC Nevin-Crooks
@lovelifepoet13
@Torbaycelebrant
@lilytheleprechaun

Dani Majestic is an 11 year old aspiring author.

The daughter of an active duty soldier, She was born in Hawaii, and has already lived in 4 different states!

She loves all things Harry Potter (she is a Ravenclaw), drawing and writing.

Dani is currently writing a novel that she hopes to publish one day.

Just as wisdom is to The Owl, so is it also, to my mother. Everything I am or will ever be, is a reflection of her radiant, generous spirit. My forever everything, even in death, she will remain the surest thing in my life.

Antoinette Salge
Shē - FB writer page

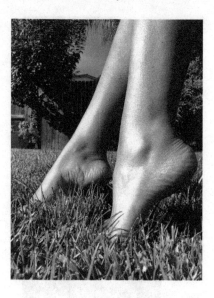

Raya Soleil is a woman who considers herself to be a free spirit, wandering far off the beaten path and following her wild heart in relentless pursuit of passion and an authentic life. Always a lover of words and stories, she began writing to help herself heal and to chronicle her process of becoming. The pursuit of authentic connections and relationships with herself and others is one of her top priorities. This project has been dear to Raya's heart as she is a mother herself in addition to having immense gratitude to the mother figures in her life. It is a privilege for her to participate in this incredible work to celebrate and honor mothers everywhere. Raya is so thankful to be able to share her journey on the road less traveled with other wandering souls through her words. It is her hope that her writing may serve to encourage, inspire, and/or amuse you while you travel through this life.

You can find more of her writing on her website: www.gypsysreverie.com or on her social media accounts: https://www.facebook.com/rayasoleilwriter and https://www.instagram.com/raya.soleil/ .

Diane McLaughlin is a Canadian born writer and poet who has been writing for over 50 years. Her passion for writing came from the desire to heal herself, as her inner voice screamed to be heard and expressed. In healing herself she hopes she helped others to heal too. She was always an advocate against abuse, especially against women and children. Today as a young senior she is very proud of her four adult children who she raised as a single parent, and her five grand-children. Diane is a "never give up or give in" kind of woman believing the best is always yet to come if you just believe.

K.G. Carroll is a poet and author residing in Central Valley, California with her husband and four children. Being a young mother and having adopted one of her daughters later in life has given her a unique perspective on what it's like to raise children on several different spectrums of parenthood. Her children have been the focus of her life and she continues to enjoy spending time with her family camping, swimming, or simply getting together for a nice meal.

You can find K.G. Carroll 's writing on Facebook at Howlings of a Dark Lonely Wolf or on Instagram at https://www.instagram.com/kry.wolf_poetry

The Messy Parts

Brenda Cierniak grew up in the heart of Lincolnshire in the UK.

From an early age writing served as a form of therapy, helping express her emotions during a traumatic childhood, and continuing to do so through the trials of adult life.

Words and their power always held a great fascination for Brenda, and poetry is an integral part of her soul. She writes from the heart, drawing on her own life experiences to write deeply personal, honest poetry encompassing; life, love, grief, abuse and mental health, with optimism and passion.

Brenda's Facebook page to share her words was started in 2020, an Instagram page following the year after.

She has published in the poetry anthology *As Darkness Falls* and the PTSDUK art book *Broken Crayons Still Colour.*

She continues to live and write in her hometown, and hopes to connect with people through her poetry.

Social media links:
https://www.facebook.com/sunshineandshadowspoet

instagram.com/sunshineandshadowspoet

Donna Blasi Miglino was born in Brooklyn, NY and currently resides in the NJ suburbs. She is blessed to be continually raised by her three (now grown) kids. A rich and sometimes twisted sense of humor, and a constantly open mind have been the most effective survival tools.

The Messy Parts

Willow Bodhi is a non binary transgender writer , artist ,energy practitioner and intuitive life coach originally from a small town in Ohio. Willow specializes in healing trauma with writing , arts and overall wellness of the mind, body and spirit . Willow is currently working on publishing their first book , and resides in Yellow Springs , Ohio with their wife and 6 children . Willow and his partner run a Non profit organization called Divine Harmony Healing Community , offering alternative healing modalities to help marginalized communities .

Best-selling author **J. Raymond** is well known for his poignant and guttural prose on subjects ranging from love, loss, death, grief, and the subtle complexities of everyday life. Nomadic by nature, but a true Southern Boy at heart, hailing from New Orleans, currently residing in San Diego. His debut collection of poetry and prose, Spades, released in February 2014, continues to reach and connect with readers all around the world. His latest work, The Kindred Project, is slated for publication in May of 2023. Once described as a "Rock & Roll approach to poetics," his honest and straightforward expressions resonate wildly with men and women unafraid of exploring the gritty and raw sides of the human experience. All of his published works are available through Amazon and Barnes & Noble.

More of his amazing work can be found online on Facebook and Instagram @j.raymond

Wendy Tobin, more commonly known as Imperfectly Perfect
By Wendy on social media, is a photographer and illustrator.
She creates illustrations for kids books as well as poetry books.
She is currently working with a few different poets on
Facebook ongoing with her illustrations and her photography.

Stacey Miller-Sommerfeld is a wedding planner and dance studio owner. She's the mom of four kids and grandma of 5 (almost 6). She began writing as a way to heal. She also loves rescuing animals and is a Freedom Transporter for her local shelter.

The Messy Parts

Danielle Gibbens can finally answer the question she has been unable to answer her whole life. You know the one: "So… what is your passion in life?" After years of searching for what it is, she can now finally answer: WRITING! When writing, Danielle feels she has finally found her calling in life. Her true north. When she writes or thinks about poetry she feels she comes alive and her real self appears.

Danielle has a great enthusiasm for writing. She looked up the origin of the word "enthusiasm." It comes from the Greek word "entheos" which means "the God within." Danielle feels by writing she has found her god, her soul, her true self within. She was born and raised in sunny South Africa before moving to England at the age of 24 where she is still trying to adapt to the cold weather 23 years later!

She started writing 14 months ago after stumbling upon an online poetry event and on the spur of the moment that night she decided to try her hand at writing and has not looked back since! Danielle has been published in "Love is Helpless" - a poetry anthology about love in all its myriad different forms and in "Immortal Tales" which is a paranormal and supernatural themed short story anthology book.

She writes mainly about mental health, love, relationships and grief and tends to write darker pieces along with a little bit of erotica now and again (it's important to mix things up!). Danielle would like to say to any other aspiring writer to keep on writing, don't give up, and to find your own god within, whomever or whatever that may be for you.

You can find more of her work on social media.
INSTAGRAM:https://www.instagram.com/her.horizon.poetry
FACEBOOK:https://www.facebook.com/DaniGirl2242

Whitney Reid is a wife and mother residing in Kentucky. She hopes to teach Elementary Education as she draws closer to her graduation date and has a strong desire to be a reading teacher. Whitney has always shown an interest in reading and writing as well as teaching. She used to create a classroom out of propped up stuffed animals (and any willing human participant) as a child and she also enjoyed writing and illustrating her own stories by using blank books. In the fifth grade Whitney won a writing essay contest and was awarded fifty dollars and a picture with the Mayor. Needless to say, it should have been obvious that her passions lay in reading, writing and teaching but it wasn't as she'd spent most of her life trying to figure out her path and true calling. Whitney realized in 2020 that it was time to reconnect herself to those passions and had her first publication in the "Trails of Light" anthology the following year. She has since been published in two other anthologies released through the 300 South Publishing Company. She often strives to forge connection and understanding through her words as well as convey deep thoughts and feelings of all kinds. Whitney has a Facebook writing page by the name of "Whitney Reid, Writer" where these words can be found.

The Messy Parts

My name is **Anna Ortiz**. I am a 47-year-old mother of two. My son Maximus is 10, and my daughter Josephine Rose is 9.

I've found writing to be very therapeutic all my life, it seems. In doing so, I hope to help others heal through my work. Although I was raised in a very toxic environment, my ultimate goal in this life is to break the cycle of abuse I came from. It is a struggle some days to accept that I have done better than that which I came from.

© Poetry & Photo Anna M. Ortiz 2023

You can find more of my poetry on my Facebook writing page:

Lost In The Background

Athena is a Wisconsin native who found an outlet in writing while navigating a complex mother-daughter relationship. After the passing of her estranged mother in 2017, her mental health took a turn for the worse and she entered a depressive episode that lasted five years. During this time she was able to use writing to help her guide her way through complex childhood trauma and grief.

She ultimately discovered her true passion in the art after realizing how much it had helped her process, heal, forgive, and find inner peace. She hopes in writing her story that it can help others find healing, forgiveness and inner peace of their own.

You can find more of her work on
Facebook: Athena Twila Poetry
Instagram: @athenatwilapoetry

The Messy Parts

Samantha Young is a passionate and dedicated mother, grandmother and writer. Inspired by her inquisitiveness, enthusiasm, playfulness and the magic, mystery, and mayhem that we call life. She has Thirty-Nine years' experience of being human traveling, exploring, and navigating this place we call earth. Hurtling through the deep dark expanse of space at 67,00 mph sharing life, experiences, and consciousness with over 9 million other species. Fumbling her way around, indulging in triumphs and defeats, adventuring, studying, experimenting, learning, growing, parenting, sharing and co-creating in an attempt to understand what being human really means.

Her writing is relentlessly real and raw, an eloquent and authentic representation of herself, her soul and her life experiences. She hopes to empower and inspire others with her unique wisdom, imagination, and truths.

Teresa Price is a rockstar wife to her husband, a dedicated mom to her three beautiful daughters, sister to four siblings, and favorite auntie to many nieces and nephews. Teresa grew up in the foothills of California's Amador County in a tiny town called River Pines. The town may be small, but her heart never stopped growing as she has always been called to be a natural caregiver, raising her children and then taking extra special care of adults with mental and physical disabilities. She has a high level of compassion and understanding for those with various challenges and finds joy in helping them reach their full potential. She loves the ocean and spending time with her family.

The Messy Parts

Hello my name is **Joshua Morales** and I'm from a small town called Lamesa. Tx. I'm obsessed with finding out who people really are.

In my occupation as a General Contractor I meet new strangers on a day to day basis and when entering one's home, conversation tends to get personal. I easily tune out those that boast on all their achievements, simply because just about anyone can be successful. All one must do is work hard at what it is they want in life. They can't teach me.

How one truly gets to know another, is if one confesses their shortcomings , their wrong doings and failures,from those i learn.

I understand things without it being shown. That's what words do for me, so I put a few of them together to try and explain to you what the most important women in my life means to me.

"Words do not, especially from a male, do anything to describe the beauty and sacrifice, the highs and lows, the sheer passion and other one million experiences that make up the mind blowingly amazing truth that is childbirth and motherhood. I am down on one knee in reverence to all women, now and always for this reason alone. I am truly humbled to be included in this sacred celebration of the same."

~**Sabian Blade**

Leigh Webb is a mom of two boys and married to a retired Marine and Sheriff's Deputy. Her youngest son is on the autism spectrum and has a dual diagnosis of epilepsy.

TK (IG: @impressions_in_ink)

Tk is 36, and has been writing seriously for 2 years. He gets most of his inspiration from video games, anime, and music.

Jennifer Torvalson is a former Rehabilitation Practitioner who has been employed in several capacities including inner-city counselor, personal aide and IPP writer for funding submissions. Privately however, she has woven words into prose and poetry since her youth. Prompted by a transformative life event late in 2021, she began openly sharing her pieces. She has gone on to publish in the poetic anthologies:(2022) Trails of Light, A Touch of Temptation, Memories, Love Is Helpless, (2023); DayDreams & Lost Wishes, Wheelsong Poetry 2, and a short story in Immortal Tales.

Although the resident Canadian is hopelessly landlocked, her writing often speaks of her ongoing love affair with the ocean and its ancient wiles.

She is a pursuer of simplicity and seeks happiness in the smallest things. When not reading or writing, she may frequently be found haunting second-hand bookstores or thrift shops and believes unwaveringly, in the beauty of imperfection.

Visit her as lostlass at seaswept7 on Instagram or via Facebook

T. B. Elden is a new writer to the poetry scene, beginning her journey in April of 2022. Writing found her after diving deep into her mental recovery, allowing her words to finally flow. Residing in Canada, she is a proud wife, and stay-at-home mother to a beautiful three-year-old girl. She loves to spend time with her family, enjoying the outdoors – whether it's a morning walk or a fun camping trip. She hopes to publish a book of some of her poetry in 2023, which will include topics around trauma and healing. Her ultimate goal is to help break the stigma surrounding Borderline Personality Disorder, and to help others realize they're not alone.

Instagram: @theborderlineempath

Facebook: T.B. Elden Poetry

Lisa Williams Freitas is the mom of four kids and ten amazing grandkids. She was born and raised in Amarillo, Texas where she currently resides with her family. She's been through her share of struggles and has had to overcome many obstacles in her life that have shaped her into the beautiful warrior that she is today. Her son, Matthew, describes her as "a lighthouse and a beacon, someone who is always there for others."

Annie Armitage is a single mum to a toddler, working full-time in risk management at a hospice. Having left an abusive marriage last year, she and her son are now building their new life together and learning as they go. Originally from the Midlands, UK, Annie and her son now live in South Yorkshire and both have an innate love of music and books. Annie uses poetry - reading and writing - as part of her recovery, and writing poetry, she realized a rebirth in her as a woman and a mother, and it's helping her find herself again.

Stephanie Houltzhouser writes poetry, and short stories. In her everyday life she is advocating for her son with autism and multiple disabilities. She is a lover of expression and believes that being sensitive only makes you stronger. No matter the way it is expressed.

Rebecca Torres a native to Austin, Texas, now resides in the Dripping Springs area. A mother to two daughters ages 19 and 22. She now spends her days reading, writing, and fighting crime with her sidekick Shi Tzhu, Douglas.

Christina Miner - I just celebrated my 40th wedding anniversary. My husband and I love to bike, paddleboard, camp and hike together. I am a mother of 3 adult children, now 5 including my married children too, and 5 grandchildren. I am a teacher and have taught in traditional, private, and charter schools. I was a homemaker and also homeschooled my own children. Other than spending time with my family, I love reading, leading small group Bible Study, quilting, gardening, and painting.

James Wesely is an American poet. His poems can be found on Instagram @vetpoetsociety.--

"On the rare days where I feel like I'm winning at motherhood…

I feel like I'm losing at everything else.

We're all just doing the best we can

and counting every small victory

as a win."

~Samantha W.~

The Messy Parts

A Word From Samantha

Truly words cannot describe how much it means to see this beautiful labor of love come to life. I had this idea for a book about the hardest parts of motherhood in my head for a while, but had no time to execute it (because I'm a tired and busy mom). Like most things, the idea played in my head on repeat, especially during meltdowns, times of frustration, and just daily mom life.

Upon a fateful conversation with Lola in December of 2022, she had the brilliant idea of putting together some kind of anthology with other writers. We went back and forth about our unique experiences as moms of kids with special needs and all of the fun/crazy things that go along with that. We felt seen and heard knowing we both knew the very real struggle of motherhood behind all of the societal filters, and unrealistic expectations.

The Messy Parts was conceived in love at that time: two exhausted moms connecting across the country, thanks to social media.

I can honestly say that it was only because of her motivation and dedication to seeing this through that I was able to keep going and make this happen. I am so thankful our paths crossed.

We were also blessed to have so many amazing contributors share their beautiful stories of love, laughter, and loss along their motherhood journeys. We truly are all connected in so many ways.

Additionally, I'm thankful for my own mother and how much she sacrificed while I was growing up. It hits differently when you're a mom, and my appreciation for her is endless. I'm also very fortunate to have a mother-in-law that is accepting and supportive of me, as I struggle through motherhood most days. Finally, I have limitless love and gratitude for my own children. They are teaching me more about life and unconditional love, than I could ever teach them…

And for that, I am eternally grateful.

The Messy Parts

Lola Lawrence is an author, life coach and mother of 3 sassy children. She has a Bachelors of Science in Behavioral-Social Sciences/Psychology. Lola writes poetry, prose, erotica, and other stories. Her debut poetry collection, Alchemy in the Dark, was released in November of 2022.

Lola is an advocate for her children who all have autism and ADHD. Her twins also have cerebral palsy. While life can be chaotic, Lola makes time for photography, painting and writing.

Lola's book, *Alchemy In The Dark* can be found on Amazon.

Samantha Woodbeck is a wife, special needs mom, teacher, and homeless youth coordinator. She is a California native, but lived in Hawaii for a few short years. She lives with her awesome husband and two crazy, amazing children, and many animals. She's easily distracted by the sky, loves the ocean, and wants to adopt all the animals.

She holds a bachelor's degree in Liberal Arts, a Multiple Subject Teaching Credential in the state of California, and a master's degree in Education.

She released her first book of poetry and prose, *Words of a Feather* on 2/22/22, and her second book, *Fractured Heart, Mended Soul* on 11/22/22. Both can be found on Amazon.

You can find more of her work on Instagram and Facebook
@Soul_Spilled_Sentiments

JUN 0 7 2023

Made in the USA
Coppell, TX
26 May 2023

17329266R00111